Praise for *Apocalypse How?*

'Entertaining and insightful . . . The picture [Letwin] paints is bleak as he uses chapters that alternate between a fictional depiction of chaotic meltdown in the year 2037 and analysis of the real-life causes to show why such disaster could occur.' **Evening Standard**

'Timely . . . it provides an insight into the mindsets that prevent politicians and civil servants from properly preparing for catastrophes.' **New Statesman**

'A vital guide for anyone in business or government who wants to know how to respond when apparently distant and implausible events strike home.' **Prospect**

'A vivid and engaging account of how the risks inherent in our increasing dependence on technology could someday coalesce into a perfect storm with disastrous consequences. *Apocalypse How?* reads like a dystopian thriller, but makes it clear that the dangers are very real.' Martin Ford, **New York Times** bestselling author of *The Rise of the Robots*

T0159835

About the author

Sir Oliver Letwin was MP for West Dorset
from 1997 to 2019. He has been an academic at
Cambridge and Princeton universities, an investment
banker and a cabinet minister at the top of the UK
Government. For six years he was a member of the
National Security Council as the minister with
responsibility for the UK's national resilience.
He lives in West Dorset and London.

APOCALYPSE HOW?

TECHNOLOGY
and the
THREAT *of* DISASTER

oliver letwin

Atlantic Books
London

First published in hardback in Great Britain in 2020 by Atlantic Books,
an imprint of Atlantic Books Ltd.

This edition published in 2021.

10 9 8 7 6 5 4 3 2 1

A CIP catalogue record for this book is available from the British Library.

Paperback ISBN: 978 1 78649 688 1
E-book ISBN: 978 1 78649 689 8

Designed and typeset by EM&EN

Printed in Great Britain

Atlantic Books
An imprint of Atlantic Books Ltd
Ormond House
26–27 Boswell Street
London
WC1N 3JZ

www.atlantic-books.co.uk

CONTENTS

ABBREVIATIONS

CCS	Civil Contingencies Secretariat
CDS	Chief of the Defence Staff
COBR	Cabinet Office Briefing Room
comms	communications
Defra	Department for Environment, Food and Rural Affairs
GCHQ	Government Communications Headquarters
GNSS	Global Navigation Satellite System
GSM	Global System for Mobile (Communications)
HMG	Her Majesty's Government (UK)
IP	Internet Protocol
MoD	Ministry of Defence
NGO	non-governmental organization
NHS	National Health Service
NSC	National Security Council
Ofcom	Office of Communications
Ofgem	Office of Gas and Electricity Markets
Ofwat	Economic regulator of the water sector in England and Wales
PM	Prime Minister

PEOPLE IN THE STORY

The Prime Minister (PM) of Her Majesty's Government (HMG), UK

General Sir Andrew Ark *Chief of the Defence Staff (CDS)*

Rt Hon. Jane Baldwin MP *Chancellor of the Exchequer*

Rt Hon. Sir Eric Bullient MP *Minister of Housing, Communities and Local Government*

Dr Bill Donoghue *Duty Officer at the Bank of England*

Dr Elaine Donoghue *Accident and Emergency (A&E) Consultant at Yeovil Hospital*

James Farrar-Scott *Duty Director at Government Communications Headquarters (GCHQ)*

Professor Dame Sheila Hart *Chief Executive of the Office of Communications (Ofcom)*

Rt Hon. Charles Hoare MP *Business and Energy Secretary*

Rt Hon. Simon Holt MP *Minister for the Cabinet Office*

Mrs Mary Hughes *mother of Dr Elaine Donoghue*

Rt Hon. Frank Jones MP *Health Secretary*

Aameen Patel *Highways England traffic controller*

Rt Hon. Liz Row MP *Foreign Secretary*

Jan Sikorski *Deputy Director at the Civil Contingencies Secretariat (CCS)*

Rt Hon. Harold Stuart MP *Defence Secretary*

Sir Jon Whewell *Cabinet Secretary*

PREFACE TO THE PAPERBACK EDITION

The hardback edition of this book was published in a different, more comfortable, pre-Covid-19 world. The global crisis through which we have all been living since that time has changed many things – some of them, in all probability, permanently. But there is one thing that it hasn't changed at all. The frenetic efforts of governments, businesses and communities to address the challenge of the virus have done nothing to resolve – have, if anything, further obscured – challenges that are only a little further off.

Although this is entirely understandable, and perhaps temporarily inevitable, it exposes us (with crushing irony) to the very same danger that has afflicted the whole world in the face of the coronavirus: the danger of being under-prepared for an event whose colossal impact is ignored because the likelihood of it happening today or tomorrow is low. Once again, both the world's leaders and the world's populations are focussing on the present. Once again, we are paying far too little heed to building resilience against the threats of the future.

This book is about one of the most obvious, but also one of the most neglected, future threats: the threat of network collapse. It presents strong reasons for believing that we need, now, to guard against this threat, and to do so in a way that is flexible, formidable and foolproof.

Much of the book is just as applicable to the world's past lack of preparedness for Covid-19 as it is to the world's current lack of preparedness for network collapse. A large part of the analysis is devoted to explaining why we all (governments, businesses, media, people at large) find it so difficult to consider small probability, large impact threats with the seriousness they deserve – until they actually arrive on the scene, at which point we spend so much time and effort attending to the current catastrophe that we run the serious risk of ignoring the next threat along the line.

So part of the point of the book is to urge that we should learn the lessons of history in the right way. Instead of assuming that the next crisis will be substantially the same as the last one, or that we have now 'had' crises, we should assume instead that a series of crises (each, in themselves, unlikely but serious in their impacts) will come at us – generally from unanticipated directions.

We should assume that our defences against them, how-ever well-constructed, will sometimes prove inadequate, because we cannot expect to construct adequate defences against unanticipated causes.

None of this, however, should make us pessimistic, let alone despairing. On the contrary, the moral of this book is that if we take appropriate steps to prepare our-selves for dealing with crises that have occurred despite our best defences against them, then we can in fact get through them with reasonable aplomb. The art of crisis management is to have means to hand of mitigating the problems we cannot prevent, and of being well prepared to deploy those mitigations in the face of disconcerting circumstances. There is no rule book, no text book, no recipe that will provide all of the answers in advance. Life as we know it in peacetime cannot be preserved, unaf-fected in wartime. But we can get through most kinds of war without too many dead at the end, if we know how to make do and mend, and if we have had the foresight to furnish ourselves with the rudimentary means of doing so.

It is in this spirit that I hope the recommendations made in this book for the construction of analogue fall-backs to handle digital crises will be read and understood. They are, I believe, a necessary feature of any resilient society in a modern age hugely dependent on a network of networks. But they are also a paradigm for the sort of preparation that humanity at large, and each country's government in particular, should make for dealing with events that we hope not to witness, may never witness, and yet which need to be recognised as possibilities rather than dismissed as fantasies.

Oliver Letwin
October 2020

PROLOGUE

Midnight, Thursday 31 December 2037

Aameen Patel may have been the first person to notice. Everyone else in Integrated Traffic Control at Highways England's Swindon HQ was either snoozing or drinking coffee in the lounge area. But Aameen had arrived at 23:45 for the midnight to 06:00 shift, and had just turned on his screen. He cursed silently when it went blank. With all this advanced technology, why couldn't they make sure computers worked on New Year's Eve?

He obviously couldn't report the fault using the normal Skype-view on his blank terminal, so he reached for his i16 to call the IT people. He was so focused on trying to remember the number that he didn't at first take in that the signal-indicator wasn't showing any bars.

It was at this point, he later remembered, that the

lights in the Control Room went off. And he realized there was some noise missing. He gradually worked out that the missing element was the usual soft hiss of the warm-air system coming up through the underfloor vents. Then, just a few seconds later, the noise of the warm air and the lights in the Control Room came on again as the reserve generator cranked into action. And that was when he looked out of the large viewing-window in front of his console. Where there should have been a thin stream of New Year's Eve traffic passing along the M25 in an orderly sequence, there was instead a growing pile-up of crashed cars and lorries, partially illuminated by headlights jutting upwards and outwards as the concertina accumulated on the icy road.

Even Aameen, always cautious about jumping to conclusions, wondered whether all of this was entirely coincidental.

▲

Some miles away, James Farrar-Scott, the Duty Director at GCHQ in Cheltenham, was a great deal more worried than Aameen. His reserve generators had kicked in almost instantaneously when the lights had flickered off, but every one of the sixteen screens mounted on the wall of his room was showing a malfunction. Unlike Aameen, he couldn't try his personal smartphone, because it was locked up in the safe at reception that was used to store mobile devices belonging to GCHQ personnel when they entered the doughnut-shaped building; but he had tried the specially protected fibre-based phone on his desk, and had found that it – as he more than half expected – was down too.

James knew perfectly well what all of this meant. Just a few days back, he had been part of the team briefing ministers at the National Security Council on the risk that someone, somewhere, might be able to turn off a lot of things at once, using the appropriate combination of cyber-worms. Now, his own words to the NSC members were ringing in his ears: 'For years, we have been warning that more and more is beginning to depend on less and less. The Internet is no longer just a communication system. It is now the infrastructure on which every major system and utility in this country depends. And that means all of those systems are vulnerable.'

Staring at the blank screens in front of him and recalling the NSC meeting, what flashed through James's mind were all the wrong turnings that had been taken by successive governments over more than a decade: the decision not to invest in an alternative mass communication system that could operate independently from the Internet; the decision to use 5G, 6G and then 7G as the basis for autonomous vehicle control with no Internet-independent back-up; the decision to let the hard-pressed NHS and social care providers base their entire integrated patient-management system on cloud-computing; the decision not to insist on expensive back-up generation for recharging electric vehicles; and, above all, the crucial decision in the early 2020s to save huge sums of money by moving the whole of the electricity, gas and water control-systems over to an integrated 6G solution. Ever since the North Korean cyber-attack on Sony at the start of the century, the extent of the vulnerabilities had been acknowledged, and large sums had been spent on building 'walls' to protect the key systems. But no one had been willing to face the elephant in the room: what happens if the walls are breached? Now, as he knew only too well, we were going to pay a heavy price for all of those decisions.

▲

Over in the Bank of England's headquarters at Threadneedle Street in London, Bill Donoghue was going through a rather different sequence of thoughts. He was thinking about his wife, Elaine, slaving away in the A&E unit at Yeovil Hospital. Ever since the new Health Secretary had won his carefully prepared battle with the consultants and had forced them to provide what he described as 'senior cover at all A&E units 24/7', it had become clear that consultant physicians at small district general hospitals were going to have a change in lifestyle; the result was Bill's solo New Year's Eve at the Bank in London rather than around the log-fire with Elaine in their Somerset cottage.

There had been, of course, nothing in particular for him to do when he arrived at Threadneedle Street as the sole officer volunteering for duty that night. Financial institutions and markets across the world were shut for New Year. Even the Shanghai Stock Exchange and the Chinese banks – which had their real holiday at the time of the Chinese New Year – would be closed for the next 24 hours. So he had been catching up with some tedious office chores that he had put off for weeks: filling out meaningless online timesheets required by some pedant in administration. He was making progress, aided by the box of Christmas chocolates he had brought in. But then the lights went off and the computer screen went blank.

The strange thing was that, when the reserve generator kicked in and the computer started up, the online timesheets didn't re-appear. He pushed every button he could think of, then re-booted the computer and finally tried to open up the FaceTime function which the Bank now used for all calls, in the hope that someone from the IT department might be around. When none of this worked, he concluded that the brief outage must have done some permanent damage to the machine and reached for his smartphone to call the switchboard. There was no signal. He realized that something quite serious had happened to the communications system.

This was also the moment when he began to worry about his 92-year-old mother-in-law, Mary Hughes. Although frail, she remained fiercely independent and had stayed with him and Elaine over Christmas. She had then returned to her own house in East Coker and had absolutely refused to have anything to do with a New Year's Eve celebration, which she regarded as arrant nonsense. So now she was all alone. If something had gone wrong with the phones, and if whatever it was had affected Somerset as well as London, how was anyone going to know if she needed help? He recalled the trip to A&E following Mary's unwise skating adventure two years ago. He really didn't fancy a repeat of that nightmare.

The natural thing would be to get hold of Elaine. But he didn't have any way of doing so. And if there really was a problem in Somerset, then her phone would be down too. This left him with the question, should he abandon his pretty well useless post at the Bank and drive down to East Coker? Or remain here and hope for the best so far as his mother-in-law was concerned? The more he thought about it, the clearer he became that he'd better go down to the West Country. With Elaine stuck at the hospital, and no one else looking after Mary, he might be needed – and he could always come back up to London well in time for the market opening in Shanghai late the next night. He headed for the internal circular yard by the Governor's entrance in which, as a special favour on New Year's Eve, the security men had let him leave his car.

As he switched on the car and turned up the heating, the thought did cross his mind that whatever was causing a problem with the phones and computers might also cause some difficulty for his journey. But, by now, he was committed to a course of action and he had never believed in vacillating: in for a penny, in for a pound. As he turned down Cheapside, he noticed a warning light on the dashboard that he hadn't seen before, and which didn't mean anything to him. But the car seemed to be working fine, and it couldn't be a battery problem because – having invested in a Jaguar equipped with the new Dyson 888 solid-state batteries – he had more than 850 miles of charge, enough to get him the 150 miles to Somerset and back and still leave plenty of spare battery for whatever he needed to do once he got there.

With almost no traffic on the London streets, everything went smoothly until he was getting close to the Hogarth roundabout at the approach to the M4 and switched on the onboard guidance system. This was when he understood the meaning of the persistent dashboard warning light. The flashing words on the screen, 'Guidance System Offline', didn't really surprise him, now he came to think of it, because he had seen the Transport Secretary being interviewed on TV just before

Christmas about some Parliamentary Select Committee report that had warned about the possibility of log-jam on the motorways if the GPS, Galileo and 7G systems failed. The Transport Secretary had been very reassuring, explaining that, although this was theoretically possible, the chances of the satellite-based systems and all of the 7G system failing simultaneously were fantastically low. Yes, he'd said, there could well be localized failures, but even these were likely to be very rare given the amount of redundancy in the systems. And in any case they would only ever cause the same sort of disruption as an accident or road closure of the sorts to which we had become accustomed over many decades.

It did cross Bill's mind at the time that the Department for Transport might have been a trifle too optimistic about this. But, however localized or generalized this particular problem might prove to be, the immediate difficulty was that, without logging his car into the on-route motorway guidance system, he wouldn't be able to enter the motorway. Or at least that was what was meant to happen. As the notices all the way from Chiswick made abundantly clear – with highly expressive diagrams for the benefit of any non-English-speaking tourists – failure to log in would cause his engine to be automatically slowed down and then shut off on the approach road.

The strange thing was that he *was* now on the approach road, and none of this seemed to be happening.

Like the smattering of other cars on the road, he seemed to be moving along, and he still seemed to be able to control the speed. Presumably, whatever system it was that was meant to stop his engine had also failed. But did this make it legal to use the motorway without logging in? Bill had no idea what the answer to that one might be. As he didn't want to run the risk of finding out, he moved into the left-hand lane and made his way off the M4 approach road onto the old A4. Clearly, other people were making the same decision; the slip road was filling up, and he couldn't see anyone in front of him heading towards the M4.

He thought it likely that he'd also be unable to enter the M25 or the M3 and would therefore have to make his way to Somerset on the A30 or some other route that didn't involve any motorways. But how to get from the A4 to the A30? Normally, it would be a doddle: just switch on the onboard guidance system, put in the destination, switch to auto-control, and the car would take him there without any further effort on his part. But with the guidance system malfunctioning, he wasn't even able to operate the plain-vanilla GPS or the direction-finding function on which he used to rely before auto-control took over. He needed to go back to the Stone Age and buy a physical, printed map. So he began looking out for a garage.

A few minutes later, he realized he had just passed a garage. Damn. Why had that happened, when he'd been on the lookout for one? He kept his eyes peeled, and then it came to him. The reason he hadn't spotted the garage was that, until his LED-light-sensitive headlights had picked up its outer perimeter, it had been invisible. And that was when he realized what he should have noticed all along. The power cut at the Bank, quickly remedied by the Bank's reserve generators, had been just a tiny fraction of the problem with London's electricity supply. It wasn't just the houses that were, naturally enough, dark at 01:30 in the morning. There were no street-lights even on the major roads where they would normally be on throughout the night; the advertising hoardings were black, and so were the garages.

In the old days, of course, there had been paper-based maps – things you could keep in the car, which didn't rely on any electronics. But no longer. Somehow, he was going to have to use his intuition and those road-signs he could read in the light provided by his headlights to find his way southwards from the A4 to the A30 and on towards Yeovil. It occurred to him that he might benefit from some traffic guidance from the BBC. So he switched on the car radio. Nothing. Clearly, with full digital switchover, whatever normally powered the BBC's transmission network had come to depend on the same source of supply that had turned off the lights, at least in the London area. Well, there was nothing he could do about any of this, so his best bet was just to continue.

1

COULD IT HAPPEN?

The events of New Year's Eve 2037, described in the Prologue of this book, are, of course, pure fiction. But are they *just* fiction? Or could they happen?

The answer is that they are *not* just fiction. They could indeed happen in any society in the developed world. In fact, there is every reason to expect that, if we don't take appropriate action, they, or something very much like them, *will* happen at some point in the not too distant future. One just has to look at the reports of the Russian cyber-attacks on Ukraine's power grid in 2015 and 2016 to see that we are dealing with a coming reality rather than science fiction.

The story told in this book is a modern-day parable: a story with a meaning, told with the purpose of conveying that meaning. But, like all parables, it is just one of many different stories that could have made the same point.

And, as with all parables, to grasp the point, one must look through the medium to find the message.

I have chosen to illustrate the fragility of converging networks, and the dangers for society of excessive dependence on such networks, through picturing what might occur if a particular event were to have a particular set of effects on the electricity grid and on certain satellites. But this is not to say that electricity grids and satellite systems are the only networks that could fail, or that an event of the sort pictured in the story is the only kind of thing that could cause such fragile networks to break down. By no means. There are many converging, fragile networks; and there are many kinds of things that could cause them to break down. The time has come to recognize that more and more parts of our lives – of society itself – depend on fewer and fewer, more integrated networks. More of our communications infrastructure, our financial and industrial systems, our transport and energy systems – in short, everything we have learned to use in every aspect of our normal lives – can now function only through a highly developed set of interconnected and interdependent networks. The electricity grid, the Internet, satellite positioning systems and mobile telecommunications networks have become the unseen net that supports the society and economy of most developed countries. And each of these networks, in varying ways, depends on the others. So we are close to having, in effect, one network of networks on which more or less everything else – government, the public services, business and family life – relies.

A good way of understanding what is going on at present – and how many of the normal features of life either already hang or will shortly be hanging on this single, fragile thread – is to think back just over forty years, to 1976. That may seem a long time ago, but it is within the lifespan of about half the people alive today.

In 1977, the launch of commercial mobile phones was still six years in the future; the Internet was in its infancy – the father of the Internet, Vint Cerf, had not yet set up the coordinating bodies that would eventually give rise to the world wide web. Most electricity supply industries across the developed world had plenty of highly flexible, fossil-fuel-generating stations which had 'black-start capability': in other words, if there was a grid failure, they could start up on their own without having to feed into the grid. There were no electric or autonomous vehicles – just drivers driving machines with internal combustion engines fuelled by petrol or diesel. There were no emails or texts or Facebook or Twitter or any other 'social media' – communication was by post, telephone or telegram: the postal system collected and delivered letters several times each day; the plain old telephone service had its own power supplies, and had no connection with the emerging Internet; the telegraph system was independently powered and totally separate from the telephone system.

Almost all financial transactions occurred either in cash dispensed by bank clerks or via cheques – interbank transfers were by telex, a system separate from post, telephone and telegraph networks. People in every service industry, including key public services, were used to receiving instructions face-to-face in offices and stations or via walkie-talkies that were powered by batteries bought in shops. In short, most developed countries had lots of separate, stand-alone systems and networks that had nothing much to do with one another. If one of them went down, the rest were likely to be entirely unaffected.

Fast-forward forty years, and most of this has changed beyond recognition. Mobile communication is now the centrepiece of life. Via the smartphone, the tablet and wi-fi, mobile networks are now completely integrated with the Internet, on which we depend not only for innumerable forms of communication but also for almost every form of information. The electricity grid's communications system can no longer be entirely isolated from the Internet. With electricity supply coming increasingly from low-carbon generators, most electricity supply industries no longer have large numbers of generating plants that can provide black-start capability in the event of a black-out caused by grid failure. Electric vehicles are multiplying, and autonomous, driverless vehicles guided partly by mobile communications through the Internet are on the way. The postal system no longer carries urgent messages on a timely basis, and relies on the Internet for its operation. The plain old telephone service has disappeared, and fixed-line communication is now all based on Internet Protocols (IP); the telegraph system has gone, as has telex. Almost all financial transactions occur electronically via IP-based systems. People in every service industry, including key public services, are no longer used to receiving instructions face-to-face in offices and stations – many of them do not have permanent offices, and they communicate for all purposes, including during emergencies, via electronic, IP-based systems. Even health services increasingly depend on the exchange of data via IP-based systems: the pace-makers in people's hearts report back continuously via mobile communication and cloud computing to the hospitals that installed them. In short, we no longer have lots of separate, independent stand-alone networks. If the electricity grid and the Internet are impaired, just about every commercial transaction and just about every activity in society is affected.

Fast-forward another twenty years to the late 2030s, and it is pretty clear that the remaining independent (and hence more resilient) aspects of our economy and society are likely to have been drawn into the same cat's cradle of interlocking systems. Electric and autonomous vehicles – wholly dependent on the electricity grid, the mobile communications system and the Internet – will be becoming the norm. Tele-health and tele-care will be

vastly more prevalent: frail, elderly people will be continuously monitored by smart technologies, as will people
with many chronic conditions. This is rapidly becoming a preoccupation for health administrators in every
advanced economy; as NHS England recently put it, 'one
of the challenges is ensuring that the way we commission,
contract and pay for care keeps up with the opportunities
digital innovation offers – ensuring that new technology is safely integrated into health and care pathways'.
Meanwhile, the use of credit cards (and hence of the
Internet) for shopping has hugely increased: for example,
more than 20% of total retail sales in the UK are already
online (almost ten times the proportion that was online
in 2006). There is every reason to suppose that, throughout the world, the proportion of financial and commercial
transactions using the Internet, either for face-to-face
credit-based transactions or for online transactions, will
continue to increase significantly in what will no doubt be
finally a cashless society. Manufacturing, energy and service industries, already heavily IP-based, will virtually all
depend on the web. The operation of government, public
services and civil society organizations will have 'caught
up' with the private sector and become net-based – and
hence net-dependent.

In short, if the electricity grid and the Internet go
down in the late 2030s, and if we have not taken very particular precautions, it is likely that life as we know it will

close down too, for as long as it takes to restore normal service. The immediate reaction of most sensible people to apocalyptic warnings of this kind is either to dismiss them as 'hyped-up nonsense' or to assume that someone, somewhere, is already 'dealing with the problem'.

But, in this particular case, there are good reasons not to regard the possibility of life as we know it shutting down as 'hyped-up nonsense' – because a sophisticated modern society is dependent on energy, transport and communication-at-a-distance to a degree that would have astonished our ancestors.

Those living in relatively unsophisticated societies of the past were far less reliant than we are today on regional, national and global interconnectivity. The inhabitants of an early-medieval manor in feudal Europe, for example, were largely self-sustaining. They grew their own crops, husbanded their own animals, drew their own water, and made their own food; they constructed (in the main) their own tools and dwellings; and they typically provided themselves with such means of transport as they possessed out of their own resources. From time to time, they might make the journey to market in a nearby town – through forests or meadows or along 'droves' or paths which they or their near neighbours maintained. But if this means of trading agricultural produce for goods from further afield was denied to them for a period of time for one reason or another, they could sustain the delay without undue disruption to the normal rhythms of their lives.

Of course, such unsophisticated societies were much less resilient than ours to events of certain kinds. They suffered from, and were often powerless to deal with, fires, floods, poor harvests, armed incursions and a multitude of ailments and diseases – including, at the extreme, the Black Death, which tore through much of Western Europe with devastating effects. The penalty imposed by the self-sustaining and simple life of small feudal communities was the inability (or near-inability) to mobilize resources on a sufficient scale and at sufficient speed to combat or respond effectively to such natural and artificial disasters. These relatively widely dispersed communities were reliant on themselves not only in the good times but also at times when they desperately needed, but could not generally obtain, help from outside.

The ability of our state and our society to respond effectively and rapidly to major events of the sort that would have overwhelmed our ancestors crucially depends on the functioning of our energy, transport and communications networks. It is these networks – national, supra-national and global – that enable us today (and even more so in the near future) to mobilize vast resources and to focus them on specific localities that need help at a given moment. The rub is that these wide-area, real-time, high-tech systems are themselves (because of their

sophistication and the wide access that they offer) vulnerable to attack from a large array of potential onslaughts,
both natural and man-made.

Although modern societies are much better protected than their predecessors against certain kinds of
danger, they are much less protected than their simpler
predecessors against other kinds of danger. On a scale
that we are only beginning to understand, our society is
built on assumptions that may be shown to be false by
events that trigger global effects. In the face of occurrences that either wouldn't have affected our ancestors
or against which they had a natural resilience, we, in our
sophistication, have lost resilience. This is exactly what
happened to the economies of the West during the financial crash of 2008: the inter-continental banking system,
which normally increases our resilience by providing
security for each individual bank, turned into a massive
liability when the failure of Lehman triggered wide-scale
effects across the financial systems of Europe and North
America.

In summary, economies of scale provide huge insurance against some forms of risk, but also dramatically
magnify others. As a result, warnings that life as we know
it could be fundamentally disrupted under certain circumstances, and that the risk of this occurring is increasing as
we become more technologically sophisticated, are far
from being hyperbole. In fact, such warnings are no more

than sober-minded observations about the circumstances we face in the not too distant future.

Nor should we assume that all is well because someone, somewhere, is 'dealing with the problem'. Of course, it is true that there are very clever and very well-informed people in positions of influence and power who do spend time worrying about these issues. And there is a widespread acceptance among those who work in the relevant fields that there are serious issues to consider. But there are also structural reasons why such issues and risks don't rise to the top of the political agenda until and unless a disaster materializes.

First, there is the doctrine of 'the more pressing question'. The business of politics, whether in a liberal democracy or a one-party state or a kingdom, is, and always has been, hugely exerting for those involved in it. Wherever you look in the world, government ministers and senior officials are busy, busy, busy. They have so many things to attend to, so many people to see, so many interests to placate, so many issues to address. They rise early and go to bed late. Therefore, they are surrounded by support systems and private offices designed to make their task more tractable by eliminating, so far as possible, all of the things that aren't a priority at any given time: to make maximum space for careful consideration of those things which are genuine priorities at the time in question. The result is that long-term dangers – things that almost certainly *won't* happen today or tomorrow – inevitably come later in the queue than the most immediate concerns. And by the time that tomorrow has come and gone, there will be some other immediate challenge which takes its place at the head of the queue. So, in any country, it is incredibly difficult to raise sustained interest in the highest reaches of government about risks that are far off.

Second, there is the doctrine of 'the reality of certainty' – in other words, the contrast between the things you can be sure will happen and the things that only *might* happen. If people at the centre of governments are busy, if resources (both intellectual and financial) are limited, if pressure for immediate results is great, then the natural response is to focus on problems that are 'real' rather than 'hypothetical': problems that you can see right before your very eyes rather than problems you might have to speculate about. Inevitably, the proposition that, at some unknown date, we might be exposed to some unknown form of attack or natural event that will have some (albeit possibly widespread) effect on our lives sounds very much like speculation rather than a fact. The natural response of the system is to leave such speculation to people in some basement or back-room and to concentrate the time and effort of senior officials (and the money that only they can mobilize) on more immediate, more certain challenges.

Third, there is the doctrine of 'the invisible benefit'. The sad truth is that, if you are a government that succeeds in preventing a disaster from occurring, the wider population will probably be unaware that it might have occurred. In many ways, this is the most powerful obstacle to serious action in the field of resilience planning. People engaged in politics the world over are hugely reluctant to spend much of their time doing things for which they will never be thanked. If the things you do or argue for have only a negative effect of preventing something happening which would have adversely affected people, then you can be quite sure you will never be thanked. No one will see disasters that don't happen and no one will know that you have done anything to stop them from happening. Invisible benefits are at a discount in politics.

Fourth, there is the doctrine of 'the unknown consequence'. This is a really hideous irony, which amplifies the problem of the 'invisible benefit'. It arises from the fact that when you take action to prevent some future possible disaster from occurring, you don't know whether the thing you have done (in order to prevent disaster) will actually *work*. You may well discover in due course that everyone *does* get to know about the ghastly event that you thought you were preventing – because you have failed to prevent it. And, at this point, you can be sure that (instead of thanking you for having tried to prevent it) the people who are affected by the event in question

22

will immediately and very forcefully excoriate you for having done such a bad job of preventing it. Worse still, because it was you who took on the job of trying to prevent it, they will specifically blame *you* rather than someone else who might have prevented it (or perhaps even had primary responsibility for preventing it) but who was lazy enough or wise enough to leave the job to you. No one is ever forgiven for a good deed that goes wrong.

Finally, there is the doctrine of 'the riper time'. This is the particular speciality of the experienced bureaucrat. It consists in explaining why 'although there is clearly much merit in taking action designed to prevent future disaster, it is in the nature of the future that it is not in the present', and that 'there will therefore be time enough, anon, to deal with such matters', and finally that 'it would accordingly be somewhat foolhardy, minister, to put this particular pan on the front burner just at present'. This is, of course, a variant of the doctrine of 'the more pressing question'. But it is in some ways subtler and more insidious because it does not depend upon the idea that it is more *important* to deal with what is immediate rather than with what is far off – just that it is not *necessary* to deal now with what can just as well be dealt with later. There may, after all, come a *better* time to deal with it, may there not?

Each of these doctrines is implicit rather than explicit. There isn't any government or international manual or guidance or diktat or speech in which such doctrines are officially spelled out or even implicitly admitted. But you only have to talk to officials or ministers in almost any front-line government department in almost any country to hear them saying things that reveal the extent to which they are in the grip of such doctrines. And the effect is that the amount of time and energy that governments spend on the resilience of systems and networks is strictly limited, even in countries that take these issues most seriously.

It is important to distinguish, here, between preventative security and the construction of alternatives. A great deal of time and money is being spent on preventative security, in the UK and elsewhere. For example, large sums are invested annually in cyber-security and in flood defence in many countries across the world; and some of the cleverest and most knowledgeable people in the world are employed in these fields. This is, of course, very important. We need to reduce the chances of damage to our infrastructure and disruption of our ordinary lives by man-made events such as cyber-attacks and by natural causes such as flooding and space weather. The building of serious defences can make a real difference to the level of risk in these and other similar areas.

But strengthening our defences to make it less likely that bad things will happen is very different from creating alternatives that will allow us to continue almost as normal if (despite our defences) bad things do happen. And this is where the five 'Doctrines of Delay' tend, above all, to kick in. It is one thing for a minister or senior official to be able to point to things that have been done to shore up our defences, and quite another for the same person to justify the establishment of some obscure fallback system that will be needed only if the defences are penetrated. In the first case, you can point to some relatively glamorous and exciting action or entity: a new National Cyber Centre, a new flood-wall or a new river-catchment management organization. Whereas, in the case of genuine fallback planning, all you can point to is some rather Heath-Robinson-like, old-fashioned, 'make-do-and-mend' fallback solution that has been organized just in case all the defences should prove insufficient to repel the natural or human antagonist. Where is the joy in that?

Does any of this matter? If the defences are penetrated, will the effects of switching off a modern sophisticated society, for whatever time it takes to switch things back on, really be *that* bad? The answer has to be that this depends on circumstances that are outside of our control. In half of the chapters that follow, I continue the story of the fictional events of New Year 2038. In this story, I picture just one plausible set of circumstances in just one country, in which the switch-off might matter very much indeed. But it is important to remember that the story that follows is just one of the many plausible stories that could be told about many possible times and places in the future. We are not dealing with one particular chain of events in one particular location. Rather, we are dealing with a set of problems that could be triggered by any number of different causes – and with any number of different potential effects, depending on the background conditions at the time when the events occur.

The sad truth is that all networks are intrinsically fragile – precisely because they are networks, and therefore depend for their operation upon the integrity of the system as a whole.

So, while our story is not a prediction, it is also not a fairytale. It is an illustration, an indication of what might be. Its purpose is not to entertain or amuse. Its purpose is to sound a wake-up call – to make clear that the increasing power, pervasiveness and interconnectivity of the modern, high-tech networks on which we increasingly rely will carry with them increasing risks for our economy and our society.

In an important recent book entitled *Meltdown*, Chris Clearfield and András Tilcsik explain in very clear terms the nature of the fragility of these key networks. Drawing on the work of the American sociologist Charles Perrow, they identify two characteristics that make any system particularly vulnerable to disaster.

The first of these is complexity – which, as Clearfield and Tilcsik point out, is quite different from sophistication. You can have a highly sophisticated process or system that is nevertheless quite simple in the sense of being linear and transparent. Clearfield and Tilcsik give the example of a modern car-assembly line, which has all sorts of very sophisticated machinery on it; but the process is linear, because each stage of the sophisticated engineering is completed before the next stage commences; and it is transparent because one can see very quickly if there is a problem with a particular stage. The proto-cars completing that stage will either be stuck, causing a log-jam that all can see, or will be entering the next stage in the wrong condition. By contrast, in a complex system, lots of different things will be going on at once, and they will be interacting with one another. Often enough, if a little thing goes wrong in such a complex system, the interactions, iterations and feedback-loops will be occurring and reverberating in a way that makes it well-nigh impossible for anyone to spot what is going on until an enormous amount of damage has been done. Even then, one may be able to see the damage and its possible causes only through indirect measuring tools, which may themselves have been affected by the complex of reverberating interactions and may therefore be giving highly misleading information. As a result, a truly complex system will typically be anything but transparent: it may take hours, days or even weeks to get to the bottom of what has been happening.

The second feature of systems that Perrow identified as a cause of fragility or vulnerability is what he called 'tight coupling'. By a 'tightly coupled' system, he meant one in which what happens in place P_1 at time T_1 within the system is likely to have more or less immediate ('real-time') effects on what will happen at place P_2 or P_3 or at time T_2 or T_3 within the same system. Clearfield and Tilcsik give a beautiful example of a university as a system which is complex (with lots of things going on at the same time that eventually and rather mysteriously interact with one another) but which is *not* tightly coupled because the causes only slowly bring about the effects, and there is consequently time for everyone to catch up with what is going on and to change direction if it looks like the wrong kind of thing. By contrast, in a tightly coupled complex system like a computer or an aeroplane the damage done by some small event in one part of the system at one moment can ripple through the whole system at lightning speed, leaving the system operators way behind.

Modern, convergent networks are classic examples of systems that are both tightly coupled and complex. Such networks typically derive much of their power and effectiveness from the fact that they contain multitudes of invisible interactions, iterations and feedback-loops. They rely on these interactions, iterations and feedback-loops occurring at the speed of electricity, which is the same as the speed of light in most non-organic networks. So they depend utterly upon system integrity. Everything has to function just about perfectly for anything to function at all, because everything relies on everything else . . . and in real time. The poor old operators have to rely entirely on highly sophisticated monitoring and measuring devices in order to find out what is happening in the network. And these monitoring and measuring devices may well be sent into various (potentially non-transparent) kinds of tail-spin by the occurrence of the very things that they are meant to be monitoring and measuring. So the operators may take a long time to catch up, and even longer to put right what has gone wrong once they know what that is.

Of course, one can seek to minimize the risks posed by this intrinsic reliance on system integrity. That is exactly what clever network-engineers try to do. For example, engineers often arrange networks so that they are 'self-healing'. If a particular route is blocked in a way that compromises the integrity of the network as a whole, such self-healing systems permit the network to find another route that bypasses the blockage. The cleverest example of all is the way that package-switching in the Internet allows tiny packages of data to travel in myriad different directions before magically meeting up and reconstituting themselves into a bit of information at the desired end-location – thereby bypassing any number of blockages that may in any millisecond have been caused by the crowding of particular parts of the network.

But these (sometimes mind-blowingly complicated and clever) techniques can never remove the intrinsic fact that a modern, convergent network is likely to be a complex, tightly coupled system, and that any form of damage which sufficiently and simultaneously disrupts parts of it may compromise the integrity of the system as a whole, and thereby compromise the operation of the network as a whole.

This is not just true of electricity grids and satellite systems. It is true also of other major networks on which modern life depends: the telecom networks (both fixed and mobile) and the Internet that allow us to communicate; the data networks on which the banking system relies; the energy networks other than electricity on which the distribution of oil and gas rely; and the transport networks – road, rail, air and sea – which permit travel to occur. Each of these systems is vulnerable, and the vulnerabilities are magnified all the time by the increasing convergence of these networks. Indeed, one can regard convergence simply as a further complexity that 'tightly couples' networks together in real time – to produce a network of networks that is even more complex, even faster moving, even less transparent, and therefore even more fragile and vulnerable than any one of the networks would be individually.

What is more, each of these complex, tightly coupled networks – even if considered in isolation, and without reference to the increased vulnerabilities arising from convergence – is exposed to a wide range of different kinds of attack, both natural and artificial. At present, the most high-profile risks probably arise for the telecom networks and the Internet, and come from human interference in the form of cyber-attack.

The head of the UK's National Cyber Security Centre released figures showing 800 significant cyber-attacks registered in the UK in the fifteen months up to the end of 2017, and alerted the nation to the possibility (indeed, the probability) of the UK suffering in future a so-called C1 level cyber-attack, which would cause sufficient disruption to the Internet to cripple key infrastructure in sectors such as energy and banking. This followed the cyber-attack on the UK's National Health Service (NHS) in May 2017 – which, according to the National Audit Office report in October 2017, disrupted 81 of the 236 NHS Hospital Trusts in England, as well as 595 general practitioner (GP) primary healthcare practices.

But Britain has, so far, been relatively lucky. Cyber-attacks at much more serious C1 level have already occurred in other countries around the world, creating problems many times greater than anything yet witnessed in the UK.

In February 2010, the Federal Government in Australia was subjected to a cyber-attack known as Operation Titstorm, in which many hundreds of coordinated attackers protesting against new pornography laws used the extraordinarily simple but effective technique of swamping government computer services and government offices with emails; they generated 7.5 million requests per second and brought down, among other things, the Australian parliament's website. In the USA (apart from the well-known issues surrounding possible electronic electoral interference by Russia), the Federal Bureau of Investigation (FBI) and the Department of Homeland Security (DHS) issued an alert in March 2018, warning people about what they described as a series of concerted cyber-attacks on US energy grids. The alert stated: 'DHS and FBI characterize this activity as a multi-stage intrusive campaign by Russian government cyber actors . . . [who] gained remote access into energy sector networks . . . conducted network reconnaissance, moved laterally, and collected information pertaining to industrial control systems.' This followed a massive cyber-attack on Sony's US network in April 2011, affecting 77 million users – albeit in a currently much less fundamental network than the energy grids. It is not only Western democracies that have been subject to such attacks. In 2014, following what the FBI in the USA identified as use by North Korea of a set of malware to hack Sony's computer network, North Korea was completely cut off from the world wide web. When questioned about possible US Federal Government involvement in this cyber-attack on North Korea, the US

State Department spokesman rather chillingly replied: 'as we implement our responses, some will be seen, some may not be seen'.

But the most powerful example of the use of cyber-attacks so far has been the series of incursions into Ukraine. A preliminary attack took place on 23 December 2015, leaving about 230,000 people without electricity. A subsequent onslaught in December 2016 brought down part of the Ukrainian state energy computer system and caused power cuts in Kiev. And on 27 June 2017, a much more profound and sophisticated attack closed down Ukrainian ministries, banks, airports, railways, metro systems and telecom services – a whole range of key networks. This was, unsurprisingly, attributed by the Security Service of Ukraine (SBU) to individuals acting on behalf of the Russian state; however, equally unsurprisingly, this was firmly denied by the Russian Government.

As these examples indicate, cyber-attacks on the telecom system and the Internet (which are nowadays much the same) can have effects on other key networks because these have already converged with telecoms and data nets by becoming dependent on them for their internal operations. As a result, cyber-attacks can now be used as a way of getting directly at other networks, by worming their way through the telecom systems into the operating systems (as opposed to merely the communications systems) used by these other types of network.

In principle, cyber penetration should be impossible wherever an operating system within an energy, transport or banking network is completely disjoined from the communications systems used by the operators. But 'complete disjunction' is very difficult to achieve. All too often, careless practice can lead the operators to make electronic connections of which they are themselves scarcely aware – but which fiendishly cunning cyber-attackers can discover.

It is easy to see how this can happen. To take just one example, the finance function of a utility, bank or energy company may choose to link the financial spreadsheets of the business with the operating systems that run the plant and machinery and the billing and customer interface. This looks entirely rational and is typically done in order to hoover up the operating data that links to financial turnover and profitability measures. How else would one enter the operating data into a financial model in the modern world? By employing clerks to read data off the operating systems in order to enter it manually into the financial spreadsheets? Hardly efficient!

Next, and equally obviously, the finance director wants to be able to discuss the emerging financial picture with her boss, the CEO, and with her assistant, the financial controller. So she sends a link to the spreadsheet, by email, to these colleagues. What could be more natural in the modern world than that?

But when the CEO opens up the link, he has (unbeknown to himself) just linked the entire telecom system and the entire Internet to the operating system of his utility – because the spreadsheet he has received via the Internet links, in real time, to the data from the operating system. So a sufficiently clever cyber-attacker can find a route, via the CEO's smartphone and the link it now carries, into the operations, and then start closing down power stations or making financial transfers or turning off the water supply for thousands, perhaps millions, of people.

So the risks run in both directions. The telecoms systems and Internet are at risk from the collapse of fundamental networks such as the electricity grid, as pictured in our parable. But these fundamental networks on which our society depends are also at risk from human interference through the data that telecoms can carry deep into the heart of non-telecom networks if the operators of those networks aren't very careful.

The reason why cyber-attack is so much a feature of our age is, of course, the very same connectedness of converging networks that makes them intrinsically so fragile. In a previous age, when activity was vastly more localized because it depended far less on wide-area networks, the ability to worm into one significant stronghold was a matter of importance, but it was not generally capable of creating crisis across a whole economy. Perhaps the sole exception to this was the sack by invaders of a great capital (one thinks of Rome or Constantinople), but these were events that could be brought about only over long periods of time and with the use of great armies. In modern economies, wholly dependent on converging networks, coordinated action by a relatively small number of individuals acting at a great distance from the scene of the attack can cause widespread damage to a connected set of fundamental network infrastructure; even a single individual, if sufficiently inventive, can cause serious damage.

Cyber-space has accordingly largely replaced sea, air and land as the terrain over which modern (often covert) network warfare is being conducted on a regular basis – and it is the terrain over which offence and defence is in future likely to be conducted with increasing frequency and ferocity. This hidden warfare is the equivalent of the medieval siege, Napoleon's continental system, or the hot and cold battles of the twentieth century for control of the oceans and of air-space: cyber-attack is the weapon of choice; cyber-defence is the defensive capability of highest priority. And, as with guerrilla warfare through the ages, cyber-space also offers a terrain for asymmetric warfare by non-state or semi-state participants – to be called terrorists or freedom fighters according to one's viewpoint.

It is this aspect of the fragility of networks, their vulnerability to cyber-penetration, as well as their centrality to our economy and society, that has led modern states to expend vast sums, very sensibly, on efforts to protect the key networks themselves against such attacks and to find means of responding quickly to an attack with both retaliatory and recuperative measures. But here, too, there is an intrinsic problem. Maximum security of a network against cyber-attack is achieved when access to the network is severely restricted (so that those accessing it can be vetted and then monitored), and when the secure network itself is isolated from all open networks. But this works in exactly the opposite direction from the strategies that will maximize the effectiveness and efficiency of any network – because, as the number and range of users grows through increasingly open access, and as connectedness with other networks deepens, any network will tend to generate what are called 'externalities' that increase its power. To see this point, one just has to imagine a telecoms system with just one user: not much use to anyone, as the one person can talk only to him or herself. Add another user, and the network becomes of some value. Add 6 billion users across the world, and the network becomes a transformative technology that increases trade, spreads innovation and improves productivity beyond imagination. But, as the network opens up in this way, it becomes progressively less and less secure. One user, and the security is (tritely) pretty much absolute. Two users, and the security is as high as your confidence in the other user. Six billion users, and there is not the slightest hope of being confident that none of them means to use the network to do you harm.

So it is the very features that make modern, convergent networks such an extraordinary force for efficiency, productivity, innovation and economic progress which, at the same time, make them extraordinarily vulnerable to cyber-penetration and cyber-attack. But, of course, cyber-attacks are just the most frequent and most developed of the forms of human interference with the networks on which we rely. We shouldn't be so mesmerized by the wonders of modern technology that we forget good old-fashioned thrillers.

You don't have to be a long way away from the computers controlling a network to get into the innards of the network. You can also be a human being right on site. Naturally, all of the utilities and other networks that lie at the centre of our economies take reasonable precautions to keep out agents of foreign powers and terrorists. But there are limits to what one can expect of any corporation – whether state-owned or private – that provides key items like electricity or other forms of energy or water or transport or banking for any society. These corporations are not intelligence services, and they don't run military installations. They aren't used to dealing with spies and terrorists. They have enough problems of their own trying to do their primary jobs: delivering electricity, oil, gas, water, transport and banking reliably and efficiently is no easy task. And making themselves super-secure against all sorts of highly unlikely events by continually searching for infiltrators or any existing member of their huge staff who has been 'turned' is a recipe for distracting management time, increasing costs and reducing efficiency. How are the corporation's managers possibly meant to identify potential malefactors? And what are they meant to do if they suspect someone? Turn themselves into amateur sleuths and monitor the individual in question at every second of the day? Nor is it any use trying to make the security less costly and less of an intrusion by restricting their attention to those key individuals who have regular and highly expert professional access to their central operating systems: a cleaner who is able to get into the right room in order to clean it is just as likely to turn out to be the unknown internal hacker. The person who knows how to turn off the economy, or is prepared to be recruited and instructed by someone who does, isn't going to announce himself or herself when turning up for a job interview.

Obviously, all of this has been true for many decades – the potential for 'insiders' to do terrible deeds has been present throughout history. Caesar was murdered by his closest colleagues; and it was insiders of a sort who opened the gates of Troy to the invading Greeks. But the difference now lies in the fact that the insider who can bring down one network may well be able – just like the cyber-warrior acting at a distance – to bring down all of the nation's networks at once because of the convergence and connectedness that make them all, in effect, one great network of networks (possibly with massive reverberations across our highly connected world). So it isn't just an individual employee of one corporation that poses a threat to that corporation and that network; the threat may come from an individual employee of any one of a large number of other corporations, whose operation of other networks converge with and are connected to yet other networks. And now we really are talking about looking for needles in a multitude of haystacks.

The exposure of modern networks to human intervention doesn't end with cyber-attack from outside and electronic manipulation from within – because the nature of the human intervention doesn't have to be computer-based. It may be much more crudely physical. The damage that can be done by someone with the right skills worming or tapping their way into a computer system can be replicated (or at least come close to being replicated) by well-orchestrated physical attacks, using old-fashioned methods such as explosives. These methods, of course, affect one place at a time – so they will typically not be capable of bringing down a network (and hence, potentially the national network of networks) unless they are either very wide in their effects (as in a nuclear explosion) or very well coordinated so that they affect numerous installations simultaneously. And, of course, the odds against either a nuclear attack or a well-coordinated series of simultaneous conventional explosions across a network are very high indeed. Someone has to have the means, the motive and the opportunity, and there are mercifully few actors (whether state or non-state) who could even be imagined to fall into this category at some point in the reasonably near future. But the fact that this is an extremely unlikely event doesn't mean that it can't happen. The point remains that, as with the far more likely cyber or electronic intervention, the existence of increasingly convergent networks presents the potential physical attacker with the opportunity to do far more damage to an economy or society more easily and more quickly than would have been possible in a more localized economy. The coming into existence of a network of networks therefore quite literally offers the terrorist or the hostile foreign power the possibility of obtaining more bang for their buck.

However, Mother Nature is at least as likely to be the cause of the problem. Space-weather events constitute just one of the many powerful attacks that nature can launch against our fundamental networks – with the potential to bring the networks down or to make them more vulnerable to man-made attack. The vast arena of physical space, and even our own Earth, as it rotates around its axis and around the sun, has the capacity to release forces far greater than the most devastating explosions devised by mankind. Major asteroids luckily seem to appear only once or twice in every 100 million years – though it is a somewhat sobering thought that the last serious asteroid seems to have arrived about 65 million years ago (with the effect, it is believed, of eliminating the dinosaurs). But leaving such extremes aside, nature relatively frequently releases forces sufficient to knock out networks or reduce their resilience dramatically if the location happens to be unfortunate; and, with climate change, the frequency of such events is likely to increase.

To take a very simple example, wind is a profound enemy of any network that relies to a substantial degree upon installations above ground level. We are normally inclined to think in terms of trees swaying and umbrellas suffering. But winds only somewhat stronger than this are quite sufficient to uproot trees – and evidently a wind of this kind is sufficient to bring overhead wiring of any kind crashing down. As long as the high winds are sufficiently localized, the damage to a network (even if overground) will be slight. But a more general storm is quite another matter.

Then there is flooding. In 2015–16, a fluvial winter flood of quite modest proportions was capable of taking part of northern England's mobile communications system out of commission for several days. Much more serious fluvial flooding, particularly if combined with high winds and coastal flooding (all of which have a tendency to be correlated with one another), could all too easily lead to a collapse of the electricity grid for a number of days – exactly like a Carrington event. Hurricanes in North America and the Caribbean, or tsunamis in Asia, could also have all of these effects. Indeed, the results of such powerful concentrations of strong wind, rain and wave could well be greater than the effects portrayed in our parable, because (in addition to the impacts of wind on the high voltage transmission network, and the impacts of flooding on sub-stations and transformers) the major coastal flooding caused by a hurricane or tsunami could disable a large number of power stations located along the coasts, in the UK and in many other countries – thereby causing a degree of damage to the balance and capacity of the electricity grid that could take weeks or months rather than days to repair.

Finally, in the tally of natural risks to which modern convergent networks are exposed, we should not neglect heat and cold. In principle, modern electronic systems are designed to deal effectively and smoothly with considerable ranges of temperature, and there are energy, water, banking and telecommunications networks operating perfectly successfully in both the coldest and the hottest parts of the world. So there is no reason to suppose that fluctuations of temperature, even if these become more extreme with climate change, should have any adverse effects on networks that are otherwise operating normally. But here, as in relation to so many other risks, it is the convergence and interdependence of networks that magnifies the exposure.

The stability of the computing that lies at the heart of the telecommunications and banking networks relies on the fluctuations of external temperature being counteracted by internal heating and cooling under all normal circumstances – and this heating and cooling depends in its turn on the energy networks for anything beyond a brief period of back-up fuel storage and generation. Hence, a prolonged outage in an energy network during a period when that network is normally required to counteract external temperature fluctuation, even if it has an effect only in a relatively localized area, could have wholly disproportionate results for the telecommunications or banking networks, or both, if the affected area happens to contain particularly significant computing capacity (for example, in a major financial centre). And this effect could become global in scale because of the profound interconnections between data centres in different locations around the world.

An important point to note about all of these network risks, both human and natural, is that – for the people who are managing the systems in question – the bottom-line financial consequences of any network failure that does occur are likely to be much less severe than might be expected, given the effects on the rest of us. This asymmetry of effect is caused by the fact that a few days, or even a few weeks, during which key networks fail is not likely to do much more than generate certain repair costs and remove a short period of revenue for the operators of the network in question. Imagine, for example, the financial impact of a week of total dysfunction on a telecoms network. Any repair costs will be written off as an 'exceptional item' on the accounts, with little impact on the value of the corporation if it is state-owned or privately owned, or on its share price if it is publicly listed – because the value of the equity and the share price on the stock exchange essentially measure the potential future earnings rather than the happenstance costs of a particular year. Moreover, the loss of a week's service will cause a dip of only 2% in turnover even in the somewhat unlikely event that all of the customers manage to recoup 100% of the (typically fixed monthly) fees that they have paid for the week in question. In the more likely event that the corporation is able to show that network failure was contractually a case of 'force majeure', an event beyond their control, and that no or only a limited refund is therefore payable, the financial effects will be even slighter.

In other words, network failure can cause risks for the wider economy and society that hugely exceed the financial or commercial risk for the corporation operating the network. As a result, the normal financial disciplines under which managers work will not be sufficient to ensure that the corporations operating the networks take these risks as seriously as the interests of society demand that they be taken. If left to themselves, the managers will 'under-price' the risk, and hence invest too little (perhaps much too little) in defending themselves against it. This points to the need for the regulators to intervene. In the jargon of regulatory economics, the regulators need to make the network operators 'internalize the externalities' – i.e. take proper account of the effect of outage on the rest of the economy outside their own business. Regulators do, typically, recognize that there is a need to compel operators of key infrastructure to do this. But, given the wide array of possible artificial and natural risks that can affect the stability of fragile and interconnected networks, it is no easy task for the regulators to specify what form this internalization ought to take – i.e. what the operators should do to minimize the risks in advance of the events that will knock their networks over.

The natural inclination of the regulators is to demand that the managers invest in reinforcement, strengthening or 'hardening' of the networks. This seems an obvious response to the problem: if a network is exposed to the threat that some human being or force of nature will attack and destabilize it in a particular way, the natural thing is to reinforce or defend the network to make it less exposed to such an attack. From quite simple flood defences (which essentially amount to no more than walls or earth-bunds) to complex procedures for detecting insider attacks on computing systems or for deflecting cyber-attack, there is a multitude of investment that can strengthen networks. Once the disruption of the economy (the social cost) is 'priced in', such reinforcement will frequently be seen to justify itself even in terms of traditional cost–benefit analysis, and will certainly be recommended by any intelligent regulator who is aware of the deficiencies of discounting the future costs of black-swan events that can have catastrophic consequences.

But when it comes to protecting society from the effects of other causes of network failure across a range of convergent networks, reinforcement is not enough.

In the first place, every regulator will be conscious of the huge costs of reinforcing and defending networks, and there will be the usual arguments against excessive investment in preventing improbable occurrences. But the problem goes beyond the fact that investment in network defence will inevitably be limited by cost. However much is spent in reinforcing the defences, there will always be the possibility that the particular natural or man-made attack is either of a kind that wasn't envisaged when the defences were being designed, or is more powerful than was imagined possible when the defences were being constructed, or both. No defences can be perfect. There will always be a remaining risk that the network will fail.

2

THE CABINET OFFICE

While Bill was making his way painstakingly in the deep darkness towards the A30, there was a considerable commotion going on in the Cabinet Office. At about 00:30, Simon Holt, the Minister for the Cabinet Office (whose responsibilities as a member of the National Security Council included resilience), and Britain's top civil servant, Sir Jon Whewell (the Cabinet Secretary) – both of whom happened to be spending New Year's Eve in central London – had arrived more or less simultaneously at 70 Whitehall. They had both headed directly for COBR, the Cabinet Office Briefing Rooms, which were meant to operate as the nerve centre for handling crises. There, they were met by Jan Sikorski, one of those heroes of the resistance on whom the civil service relies and whom it rarely promotes. Jan had been stuck for years as the Deputy Director at the Civil Contingencies Secretariat, not least because he knew more than any other living person about how to handle emergencies, and no one really wanted to find out whether the system could operate without him. Never once complaining about his one-star rank (though often having to deal with less competent two-star and three-star colleagues, who were Major-Generals or Lieutenant-Generals in the army or Directors or Directors-General in the civil service and the civilian agencies), Jan had maintained sanity, calm and orderly process through a series of domestic crises. But this one was testing even his nerve.

'So you are telling me', said the Cabinet Secretary, 'that the Minister for the Cabinet Office and I can contact the PM, the Chancellor, the Foreign Secretary, the Home Secretary and the Defence Secretary and a small number of other key people but cannot contact any other living soul from the Cabinet Office Briefing Room suite.'

'That is correct. Since the decision was taken to rationalize all HMG communication in 2025, and move it onto a secure version of the modern, Internet-based communications system, only the old direct analogue telephone link to the ministers you have named and the small number of other key people on that system will continue to function if the entire UK Internet and digital mobile telephone networks are down – which, so far as I can make out, they are at present. There used to be a completely separate comms system for selected ministers, departments and agencies. But the budget for that was removed when we moved onto the highly protected network – as the new network covers a much wider range of locations and has much higher specifications. At the time, the Civil Contingencies Secretariat warned that this would reduce resilience in the case of a complete Internet and mobile outage, but the risk of that occurring, in the light of the reinforcements that had been built in, was judged by the Treasury to be too low to be of concern. Your predecessor and the Minister for the Cabinet Office agreed with the PM that, despite this, we would keep a scaled down version of the old system going just for the key fifteen locations out of the CCS budget. So we are where we are.'

The Minister for the Cabinet Office, Simon Holt, wasn't surprised by any of this. His had been the lone voice in the NSC calling for measures going beyond the 'hardening' of the networks. And he knew perfectly well that, in the event of the National Grid failing – which is what he very much expected had happened – none of the back-up generation available in public buildings and major firms would be sufficient to keep the communications systems going. He was also painfully aware that the decision of the NSC not to legislate for separate back-up generation in the new mobile system, once the 5G, 6G and 7G technologies had been moved over to unmanned aerial vehicles (UAV) circling the globe, would mean that even the basic texting arrangements that had been put in place for just such an eventuality in 2020 would no longer operate. But what was really worrying him was the effect on the frail elderly. High-tech items like the nuclear power stations, hospitals and military establishments were protected by 'fail-safe' systems designed into them; but frail, elderly people were not protected by any such systems. With no electricity in their homes, and with their gas heating now entirely dependent on electric smart meters, they were going to have a very cold first five days of January while the grid was brought back into life – even assuming there was enough 'black-start' generating capability available to do that. And, without any communications system, who was going to know which of these elderly people needed help, or be able to get the help organized for them?

Although Simon Holt was inclined to like the new Cabinet Secretary (who had taken over a week earlier, on Christmas Eve), their relationship was still at the formal stage – not like the close working relationship he had built up with Jon's predecessor over the six years since the 2032 general election. Would it be appropriate, after having met on only two or three occasions, to use Christian names? Given the pressure they were going to be under together over the next few days, he thought he might as well take the plunge.

'I'm afraid, Jon, that Jan is absolutely right. When

this is all over, we must have a quiet lunch or dinner so I can tell you how your predecessor and I lost all the battles over resilience in the last Parliament. But, for now, we just have to deal with the situation as it is. I am pretty well convinced that what we are witnessing is a scenario that I have been warning might happen: I think the National Grid has for some reason failed – possibly because of a space-weather event of a kind we hadn't anticipated, rather than sabotage of a kind we had anticipated – and the failure of the grid, as well as turning off all the electricity in places not covered by stand-alone back-up generation, will have triggered total failure of the Internet and of all the communications networks. If I'm right that the underlying cause is space weather, then there will also have been effects on air traffic (though few planes are probably in flight over Europe at midnight on New Year's Eve) and, much more seriously, on the GPS and Galileo satellite systems, which will probably have been knocked out. All of this means that we probably have a transport system in chaos, and millions of old people stranded in unlit and increasingly cold homes. I think that, rather than worrying about our inability to call a proper national COBR conference, we should convene an immediate discussion with the PM and the other senior ministers who are linked into the plain old telephone system which, thank God, we have preserved for the top fifteen locations.'

'I agree, Simon. You and Jan have much more experience of this than I do; and it must clearly be right to involve the PM and senior colleagues right away. Can you set that up, Jan?'

'Of course. I will have the PM, the Chancellor, the Foreign Secretary, the Home Secretary and the Defence Secretary on a conference call within ten minutes.'

'Thanks. And now, Simon, can you use the ten minutes we have before the conference call to explain the point you are making about space weather?'

'Well, I am no expert on the science, but the practical issues are clear and straightforward. From time to time, things called Carrington events happen in the sun or elsewhere in the solar system that generate major magnetic pulses. I think this was first noticed by von Humboldt in the early nineteenth century, who saw his compass being affected when there was a meteorite shower in the sky. These events in space can have quite localized effects on Earth. In the middle of the nineteenth century, there was a so-called "coronal mass ejection" from the sun which knocked out some telegraph systems. And, much more recently during the late 1980s, a magnetic impulse from space brought down the Hydro-Québec electricity grid, without affecting other electricity grids in Canada. So we have known about these events and their possible effects in specific locations for a long time. But we haven't been able to work out any way of protecting electricity grids from them.

'Together with your predecessor and the Director of GCHQ, I tried to persuade colleagues on several occasions that the risk of space weather causing a grid failure was not negligible and that we should provide alternative sources of power for all critical functions. We also argued that we should reconfigure communications systems to work on a reduced basis with back-up power and simple texting if the failure of the grid brought down the Internet in the UK. We pointed out that this had been discussed for twenty years, that we had had a system in place for 3G/4G terrestrial mobiles, and that we needed to act now to replicate that for the 7G networks based on UAV. But we failed. We couldn't persuade the National Security Council or Cabinet that the chances of the grid being knocked over by space weather or anything else were high enough to warrant the extra cost of creating systems of this sort.

'Everyone said that we had muddled through so far, and we could probably muddle through for the foreseeable future. You know, the kind of discussion where all the sensible people are on one side, and the person pointing out the obvious begins to look like a complete madman . . . Incidentally, the reason why I think what we are now experiencing may be the effect of space weather is that this fits all the facts we know so far. As we have seen, all the comms are down. That could of course have been caused by a massive cyber-attack on our communications systems. But the lights are also off, except where there is a back-up generator, so there must have been a failure in the national electricity grid. But it is unlikely that a cyber-attack would simultaneously turn off both the electricity grid and the telecoms networks. So it seems that the comms have probably been turned off by the grid failure. We are therefore looking primarily for a cause of grid failure – and there is no sign either of extreme terrestrial weather or of a nuclear attack, which are pretty much the only two other things besides space weather that could cause grid failure of an instantaneous and completely unpredicted kind. If it were just a case of generating stations or part of the grid failing due to natural causes or terrorism or cyber-attack, there might be 'rolling brown-outs', but there probably wouldn't have been sudden black-out. Moreover, we know that the GPS satellite systems aren't working in our sat navs. So the satellites (which obviously don't depend on the electricity grid) must also have been turned off by something; and the natural cause of satellite failure (other than a military attack in space, or a fiendishly clever form of cyber-attack) would be a space-weather event. All in all, a space-weather Carrington event fits the facts. And such an event could have occurred without our having predicted it, because the satellite monitoring of space weather went wrong in the 2010s and won't be replaced by a fully robust arrangement for monitoring and prediction until 2039, because of an unfortunate series of launch failures and technology crashes. But of course I could be completely wrong about all of this; it may be that the power and comms outages are restricted to London, or that they are national but have been caused by something else that we hadn't thought of. One of the first principles of resilience planning is that you need to be prepared for things whose causes you may not know; and that is precisely what we have not done in this country (or, for that matter, anywhere else that I know of).'

As Simon Holt delivered this long monologue, the Cabinet Secretary nodded. He was remembering the briefing he had received earlier in December from his outgoing predecessor, who had warned him that, although he and Simon had succeeded in helping the PM to steer the government through a series of tricky problems, there were areas of remaining vulnerability including some aspects of national resilience and over-dependence on what he had called the 'cyber-electric nexus'. He also remembered his predecessor humorously pointing out that, in the event of systemic failure, it was always open to a PM to use the Cabinet Secretary as a fall-guy. 'And that guy now is not me, but you, Jon.'

Further musing along these uncomfortable lines was, however, interrupted by Jan Sikorski announcing: 'I have the Prime Minister on the line. Prime Minister, the Minister for the Cabinet Office and the Cabinet Secretary are with me here at COBR; the Chancellor of the Exchequer and the Foreign Secretary are joining the call; we cannot trace the Home Secretary or Defence Secretary, but I have their duty private secretaries on the line from the Home Office and the Ministry of Defence; I also have James Farrar-Scott speaking from the Director's office at GCHQ and duty officers on the line from C's office, the private office of the Director-General of the Security Service and the Commissioner's office at Scotland Yard, as well as duty secretaries from the offices of the first ministers of Scotland, Wales and Northern Ireland.'

The PM spoke first in his usual calm and logical way, setting the tone for this and all subsequent meetings on this crisis:

'Thank you, Jan. I'm grateful to all colleagues for joining this call at a late hour on an unfortunate night. Simon and Jon: as you are at the centre, could you give us your assessment of the current situation – Simon first?'

'Well, Prime Minister, we have very limited information at present. But, on the assumption that all participants to this call have the same experience of no mains electricity and no mobile phone usage or Internet connectivity, then we can say that at least in London and wide areas of the UK the electricity grid and the communications systems are down. Can I just start by confirming that all colleagues are in that position?'

There was universal consent.

'In that case, I think we should also make at least a working assumption that the National Grid as a whole is down – and that this is what has cratered the communications systems. Also, for reasons I have just been explaining to the Cabinet Secretary, it is likely that this has been caused by space weather, as we are not aware of any other likely causes of very sudden and total grid failure, apart from extreme terrestrial weather or nuclear attack, neither of which is in evidence. Prime Minister: would you like me to continue with a brief assessment of the likely consequences at this point?'

'Yes please, Simon. We cannot be sure that your analysis will prove correct; but at least it fits the facts that we know so far. If it is correct, what will happen next?'

'The first point is that the entire communications system will be down. Both the Internet and the land-based element of the 7G UAV-based mobile systems depend entirely on electricity from the grid. Also, none of the emergency service control systems will be able to contact police cars, ambulances or fire engines (even assuming their batteries last), because we decided to let all of the emergency services move over to the enhanced 7G public service network. We are now speaking on one of the very few independently powered non IP-based, legacy communications systems in existence in the UK, and this system reaches only as far as the fifteen locations at which participants to this call are located.

'The second point is that the transport system will be seriously diminished. Cars, vans and lorries that don't use their onboard navigation systems or the on-route motorway guidance systems will be able to move around cities and roads other than motorways – but only for as long as their batteries last and as long as they can find their way without GPS or Galileo. The trains will all be stationary, because the new digital switching system depends on the comms networks: you'll remember we decided not to invest in an independent network. And planes – apart from any that may have been directly affected by the space weather – will all be grounded because the air-traffic-control systems are also dependent on the comms networks.

'So far as electricity is concerned, all government buildings will have reserve generators, as will hospitals, major police stations and other emergency service depots and control centres. I wish I could say with certainty that all the reserve generators have enough fuel on site to keep them running for the five days it will take to get the grid fully up and running; but I am pretty sure that this will be patchy, despite a rain of circulars from my office over the last five years.

'But my biggest concern is with ordinary life for ordinary people over the next five days.

'In all homes the heating, whether electric or gas, is essentially grid-dependent, because it is controlled by smart meters that are grid-, mobile- and Internet-dependent. Likewise nearly all cooking is smart-meter-dependent. I say 'nearly' because obviously some people will have camping stoves and the like. Given that temperatures are close to zero at present during the day, and reach well below zero at night, the lack of heating and hot food and water is probably a much more immediate problem than the lack of lighting or communication. Even people who have solar panels or wind turbines and corresponding electricity storage systems of their own will be no better off than the rest of us – because these too now operate via the smart-meter system that depends on the grid and the comms networks (you may recall that Treasury rejected my proposal a few years ago to mandate the installation of a manual switchover for all homes equipped with in-house generation and storage). And, when it comes to buying things like candles and cold food to keep going, neither the online retailers nor the remaining shops and supermarkets will be able to make sales; as you know, when we moved to a fully cashless economy in 2027, we specifically accepted that all transactions would now depend either on mobile comms at the shop or on fixed-line Internet. That's why we had the 'Help-to-phone' programme that gave free 6G smartphones to anybody over retirement age or out of work who wanted one. Unfortunately, they won't be any use for the next five days.

'My fear, as I was saying to the Cabinet Secretary just before this call, is that we could be faced with frail, elderly people, who don't have relatives or friends living nearby, left stranded in their homes without light, heat, cooking or communications – in the freezing cold. It's anybody's guess how many of these there are – because the Ministry of Housing, Communities and Local Government rejected a proposal from the Civil Contingencies Secretariat to have all local authorities maintain a paper-based register derived from an annual survey, on the grounds that this would be an unfunded burden for councils. But my educated guess is that the number will have six noughts rather than five after it.

'I have no doubt that – whatever disturbances this episode may cause in some quarters – the Dunkirk spirit will lead to a lot of self-help and community help over the coming week. Even in the urban areas, where nobody tends to know their neighbours, people will tend to help each other in the face of shared crisis. But I very much doubt that this will be sufficient to solve the problem for all of the stranded elderly.'

Whatever might have been going on in the recesses of the Prime Minister's mind, he was not going to be put off by Simon Holt's repeated pessimism – however justified it might prove – and he was more than capable of maintaining calm in a crisis: 'Thank you, Simon; a masterly and concise summary of the difficulties we may be facing; Jon, do you have anything to add from the centre?'

'Not really, Prime Minister. The Minister for the Cabinet Office has set out a plausible working hypothesis.'

'Thank you. Let's now hear from the Chancellor of the Exchequer and the Foreign Secretary. Jane: what is your assessment?'

Jane Baldwin, who had been Chancellor of the Exchequer for just about as long as anyone could remember, had confronted almost every kind of challenge over the years. True, this was new, even for her, but she wasn't inclined to believe that all her resistance to expenditure on resilient alternatives to the main networks was going to come back and bite her so hard:

'Well, Prime Minister, I think we can rely on Simon to have illustrated the worst case very effectively. He has, after all, been warning us about this kind of thing for some years. But I wonder whether we should assume the worst at this early stage. Shouldn't we begin by trying to find out whether the National Grid has actually failed? A lot hangs on that, and at present we are dealing with pure speculation.'

At this point, there was an interruption from James Farrar-Scott, whose previous posting had been as one of the PM's private secretaries before returning to GCHQ, and who therefore understood the dynamics of these conference calls as well as any of the ministers: 'Prime

Minister, James Farrar-Scott here from GCHQ; I wonder whether I could help answer the Chancellor's important question?'

The PM was delighted to hear from a trusted and expert official. The last thing he could afford was for this call to descend into a jousting match between two of his closest colleagues, who had been disagreeing over fallback investment for years. 'Good to have you with us. Go right ahead.'

'Thank you, Prime Minister. First, the facts. We have full power via our reserve generators here at Cheltenham. All our internal machinery appears to be in working order. But I am getting no response whatsoever from any of the monitors that normally enable me to observe levels of Internet and network traffic. Nor are the GPS or Galileo systems – or our other GEO comms satellites in Europe – responding. In addition, I am getting reports on our dedicated, independent monitoring network from all our UK-based out-stations, showing that they have all switched to reserve power. Then we come to what this means. I think there can be no doubt, given what I can see and not see from the monitors here, that there has indeed been a National Grid failure – and that whatever has turned off the grid has also turned off the positioning satellites and comms satellites positioned over Europe. This could, of course, have been caused by something of which we have no previous knowledge; one cannot discount that possibility at this stage. But I am bound to say that the analysis provided by the Minister for the Cabinet Office is a good deal more than a working hypothesis. It looks pretty much like a racing certainty at present.'

'Prime Minister, I wonder whether I might chip in at this stage?'

Like everyone else, the PM instantly recognized the voice of the Foreign Secretary, Liz Row. Those gravelly tones had become known to most households in Britain over the last fifteen years of broadcasting from an MP who, in her time, had had many ministerial roles and who had done much as Foreign Secretary to build closer links with China and India. 'Certainly, Liz.'

'Thank you. As we all know, my last visit to China resulted in an agreement with the Vice-Premier to install a dedicated line between him and me.. For the purposes of resilience, it also has its own power source. And it has 'hardened' security, making it just about impossible to hack. But it does use the same IP-based system as the rest of the comms networks. Just before coming into this conference call, I tried to get through to the Vice-Premier to ask what the situation was in Beijing. Unfortunately, the line was dead. Although I was interrupted by the call from the Cabinet Office before I could make contact with GCHQ or any other experts, I think we can take it that the UK currently lacks access to the global Internet – if, indeed, the global Internet is up and running elsewhere in the world. Assuming that other countries, with separate electricity grids, still have power, and assuming also that they still have access to the Internet, then this would seem to indicate that Simon and GCHQ are right about what is going on.'

'Thanks, Liz. That is very helpful corroboration. Jane, I think you will agree that we should, at least for now, operate on the assumption that what we have heard from Simon, from GCHQ and from Liz is right – and that we are therefore probably facing the consequences of a grid failure which has caused a communications black-out in the UK?'

Clearly, this was not what Jane Baldwin had wanted to hear. But she hadn't been one of Britain's longest-lasting and most successful finance ministers on the basis of brute refusal to acknowledge facts when they stared her in the face.

'Yes, Prime Minister. I am forced to agree that Simon's hypothesis does seem to fit with what we now know. We should therefore operate on that basis. Clearly, the Treasury will make available whatever funds or spending permissions are required to do whatever is necessary to deal with this crisis.'

'I'm grateful. Now we should turn our attention to the actions we can take.' As the PM said this, he realized with a thud that he had in fact completed the easy part of the call. Getting agreement on what was happening was a doddle compared with working out what to do about it. How on earth was he supposed to run a country and keep its vulnerable people alive when he hadn't got any mains electricity or any communications to speak of? Well, best to give himself and the others some time to think about that by filling in a bit more of the picture: 'Jan, I wonder whether CCS could at this stage give us some indication of how the recovery of the grid will be managed, and how long it will take.'

'Certainly, Prime Minister. This is something that CCS has studied intensively with National Grid – and we have run a series of trials under the auspices of the Minister for the Cabinet Office.

'Basically, when the grid fails, all of our power stations and all of the elements of the electricity distribution system cut out automatically. National Grid then needs slowly to recreate the balance of supply and demand – since the grid can work only if, second by second, the same amount of power is flowing out of it as is coming into it.

'This balancing act begins by turning on a power station that has "black-start" capability; in other words, a power station that can operate without connection to any demand. The grid then switches on a corresponding amount of demand by opening up a particular element of the distribution network in an appropriate part of the country. The process from then on is jerky. From time to time, a particular patch of the distribution network will need to be switched off when another bigger patch is brought on, in order to maintain the balance of supply and demand.

'So, for about five days, as more and more generating plant is restarted, the lights in particular places will come on, go back off, and come back on again. Of course, this all depends on equipment such as the transformers not having been permanently damaged by the magnetic impulse from the space weather. If, as is likely, some of the equipment needs to be repaired, this will cause further delays in some places.

'And all of this will be made much more difficult by the fact that the comms systems on which the National Grid now depends are mainly the 7G networks that in turn depend on the mains electricity supply. The Minister for the Cabinet Office and I did persuade National Grid to invest in some very old-fashioned, battery-powered walkie-talkies from Ghana. But the energy regulator, Ofgem, refused to allow the grid to pass to customers the cost of installing a fully specified independent grid comms system, on the grounds that Treasury guidance assessed the risk of a grid failure as too low to produce a positive return on such investment. So the management and the engineers will be operating on a rather hand-to-mouth basis for the first few days. My own estimate is that we will therefore be lucky to see full restoration of the grid within the official five-day period – though I guess that there will be power by the 5th of January in many parts of the country.'

'That is very helpful, Jan. Can I turn now to the MoD? Is the Defence Secretary with us yet?'

'Yes, Prime Minister. When the power and normal comms went off, my office very helpfully organized a helicopter to collect me from Kent, and I joined your call from the MoD a few minutes ago. I think I have got the gist of the conversation so far.'

'I'm glad to hear that, Harold. I take it that all the appropriate measures will have been taken so far as our armed preparedness and the nuclear deterrent are concerned. But can you tell us what you think the armed services can do to aid the civilian powers over the next few days? It sounds like we may be depending heavily on you.'

'Well, Prime Minister, the good news is that we have never believed in the resilience of the grid. We and the Pentagon have been taking space weather very seriously for many years, and we decided a few years back to provide ourselves with a successor to the disastrous Bowman mobile communications programme. As a result of this all our forces are now equipped with mobile communications that operate on old walkie-talkie principles, with batteries that can be recharged from stand-alone generators backed up by fifteen-day fuel supplies held in military bunkers.

As you know, we also resisted calls from NGOs to move onto an electric basis for military equipment, so we are still using diesel for all land-vehicles, and we have fifteen-day fuel supplies for all the vehicles based in the UK. We also now have sufficient kerosene storage for all UK-based military aircraft. I think I can therefore say that, whatever problems you have on the civilian side, you do have armed forces available to you over the next few days. We just need to work out how best to use them.'

This was just the ray of hope the PM needed. He knew that Harold Stuart was always inclined to take a 'can-do' approach to anything. That was, indeed, why he had sent him to the MoD. And now that decision was paying dividends. But this also meant he had to ask the next question: 'Thank you, Harold. That is enormously reassuring. Could you just tell us what you meant by describing that as the "good news"? Is there some bad news to go alongside it?'

'Yes, Prime Minister. I'm afraid there is. The truth is that I don't have very many bodies on the ground in the UK. You will remember that the previous government decided to discontinue the build-up of the reserves that we had maintained throughout our last period in office. It has taken us years to restart that programme, so we have only limited numbers of reservists; the Royal Navy is essentially on the high seas; much of the RAF is stationed in the Middle East, the Falklands and elsewhere;

and a large part of the regular army is training abroad. I will have this checked as soon as I can get the relevant people brought into an MoD meeting, but my guess is that I probably have no more than about 35,000 personnel actually present in the UK. This compares with a million people working in the NHS and 1.5 million working in adult social care. So, if the main issue is how we keep frail, elderly people alive and well over the next week or so, my 35,000 is a bit of a drop in the ocean.'

3

THE SOCIAL IMPACT OF
BLACK-SWAN EVENTS

The chain of entirely possible events being hypothetically discussed at the COBR meeting described in Chapter 2 is clearly very worrying. If this chain of events were to take place, it wouldn't just be the ministers and officials gathered in the Cabinet Office Briefing Room who would be concerned about them. The entire nation would be able to think and talk of little else.

But what is the probability that the first event in the chain – the collapse of the electricity grid and of the Internet in the UK – will actually occur? The answer is, of course, that the probability of these things happening on any given day is very low. They are called 'black-swan' events because, as with black swans, they are very rare. But the fact that something is a black-swan event doesn't mean we can relax and forget about it. The temptation to do this arises from sloppy thinking. And sloppy thinking can cost lives.

In 2017, Robert Meyer and Howard Kunreuther, two professors from the Wharton School at the University of Pennsylvania, published a fascinating book called *The Ostrich Paradox*. As the book's subtitle states, the authors set out to explain 'why we underprepare for disasters'. Their explanation is that we suffer from six important mental biases: myopia, amnesia, optimism, inertia, simplification and herding. Each of these tendencies is involved in the sloppy thinking that leads people not to pay enough attention to the threat from black-swan events.

Meyer and Kunreuther attribute our myopia about black-swan events to the fact that anybody's brain treats 'rewards that are immediately present quite differently from those that lie in the imagined future'. In particular, they observe that we have a tendency to engage in 'hyperbolic discounting' which assigns too little weight to future events; and that people 'act myopically . . . because of a change in which consequences they focus on when thinking about the present versus the future'. Meyer and Kunreuther cite the very interesting evidence that residents living in the path of Hurricane Sandy were amazingly reluctant to move out of their homes to avoid the hurricane, just because of the fuss and bother that such a move would entail. Another example of the same phenomenon (not, as it happens, presented in *The Ostrich Paradox*) is the notorious reluctance of many well-off German Jews to leave Germany in time to save themselves from annihilation in Hitler's death camps: they focused on the inconveniences of leaving (which were near at hand) and therefore discounted too heavily the horrors of being exterminated (even though these were only a little way off). As Meyer and Kunreuther put it, 'decisions to invest in protective measures require powers of foresight' – and our tendency towards myopia often deprives us of that foresight when it comes to black-swan events.

The second bias identified in *The Ostrich Paradox* is our tendency towards amnesia. Meyer and Kunreuther point out that we normally learn useful skills by remembering good outcomes and by repeating the actions that cause them, which means forgetting bad outcomes and the actions that caused them. But this useful selective amnesia 'can backfire when it is used to discover the value of investing in protection against low probability, high consequence events. The reason is simple: in such contexts, successful learning requires us to reverse the natural tools we use to acquire skills in other domains . . . [it] requires us to see value in costly actions that carry few observable rewards. A successful protective act, after all, is one that leaves our lives unchanged; the benefit lies only in losses that might have occurred but did not.' In other words, the selective amnesia that allows us to make progress in normal life makes us peculiarly ill equipped to assess accurately the dangers of black-swan events.

Next, comes the optimism bias – which, in this context, is taken to be our 'tendency to believe that [we] are more immune than others to threats'. Meyer and Kunreuther cite studies showing that 'in virtually all cases, people saw their own odds of escaping . . . misfortunes as being much higher than those of others'. This, they argue, is typically combined with an 'underestimation of cumulative risk'; the result is an optimism which leads people often 'to concede that a hazard is likely to occur, but to take limited or no personal actions to reduce the potential damage'. Because of our optimism, the abstract recognition that the world in general may be affected by black-swan events does not translate into any corresponding personal fear or any personal decision to do something that will prevent the fear from being realized.

Meyer and Kunreuther argue that these powerful tendencies towards myopia, amnesia and optimism are reinforced by inertia: 'one of the major reasons why we often err when making protective decisions is that we usually prefer not to make such decisions at all . . . and to look for defaults that free us from the labors of difficult, deliberative . . . thinking'. In addition, we are subject to the sin of simplifying life by ignoring the small: our brain tends 'to process only those cues it perceives as being large and thus meriting attention – which is a particular problem for extreme events whose probability of occurring is, by definition, quite small (though with large consequences when the events occur)'.

And, finally, we are often misled by our tendency to follow the herd. In the context of black-swan events, this is a mistake because 'at least when it comes to protective investments . . . there is, as it turns out, little wisdom in crowds. People indeed have a strong instinct to look to the behavior of others as a source of guidance, but doing so often seems to intensify individual decision biases.'

All of these observations about the way we think are helpful explanations of the extent to which, in our everyday lives, we tend to underplay the risks and threats of low-probability, high-consequence events. But surely governments and bureaucracies are established to avoid such sloppy thinking? Aren't they meant to be more rational about such matters than most of us manage to be in our everyday lives?

The sad truth is that, even in highly sophisticated organizations, there are strong tendencies to make many of these same mistakes when dealing with black-swan events. The mistakes just get made in a more sophisticated way.

Part of the reason for this is that governments are not very good at being clear about the true meaning of probabilities. Indeed, probability typically plays tricks with the mind.

Take a very simple example. If something has only one chance in a *thousand* of happening on any particular day in the next three years, that might at first seem to any unwary minister or civil servant like a very small chance. But what this statistic actually means is that the thing in question has a roughly 30% chance of happening on at least one day next year, because there are roughly one third of a thousand (365) days in next year. This may at first sound counter-intuitive. But a simple thought-experiment is enough to show that it is in fact the case.

Imagine, for example, that a friend promises that he will buy me an ice cream on one specific, as yet unnamed, day at some point in the next three years. Suppose that (a) I have every reason to believe that my friend will in fact fulfil this promise but (b) I have no information on which to base a guess about which of the roughly 1,000 days over the next three years will be the lucky day. In that case, my estimate of the chance that he will do it on one day over the three years (barring death or disaster) is close to 100%; and my estimate of the chance he will do it in any one of the three years is a third of that – close to 33%; but the chance that it will happen tomorrow (being one of the available roughly 1,000 days) is only about 1 in 1,000, because the chance that it will happen on each one of the other roughly 999 days is just as high, and it isn't going to happen on more than one day in the thousand.

So the statement that a given, specified event has a chance of one in a thousand of happening tomorrow (or on any specified other day in the next three years) is equivalent to the statement that the event in question has a roughly 30% chance of happening on some day in the next year.

That sounds like a much bigger chance than 'one in a thousand'.

And even if something has only a one in a *hundred thousand* chance of happening on a particular day in the next 300 years (which sounds like a really tiny probability), this actually means that the thing in question has a roughly 3.3% chance of happening once in the next decade.

Go back to our simple thought-experiment. Suppose that my friend assures me that he will buy me (or that his descendants will buy my descendants) the rather long-dated ice cream on some day in the next 300 years. And suppose that (for whatever reason) I am almost 100% confident that this promise will be fulfilled – but that, again, I have no idea which particular day will be the lucky day. In that case, the chance (as assessed by me) that he will buy the ice cream in any particular decade within the thirty decades that there are in 300 years is 1/30th of almost 100% – or roughly 3.3%. But the chance that he or his successors will buy the ice cream on any particular day within the roughly 100,000 days that there are in 300 years is only about 1 in 100,000 because I know that the event will only happen once in the roughly 100,000 days. So the statement that there is a 1 in 100,000 chance of me or my descendants getting the ice cream on any particular day in the 300-year period is equivalent to the statement that there is a 3.3% chance of me or my descendants getting the ice cream in any particular decade over the next 300 years. This sounds like a counter-intuitive equivalence only for as long as one doesn't think about it.

In short, ostensibly tiny chances, about which one might be inclined not to worry, can often be misleadingly comforting if one doesn't look very carefully at the exact description that the statisticians or forecasters are attaching to their statistics or forecasts. One often finds that the chance of the dreaded event occurring at some unknown time is actually a whole heap more worrying – and ought to preoccupy policy-makers a whole heap more – than the ostensibly tiny probabilities of the event occurring on a particular day originally led one to suppose.

The next problem with relying on the unlikelihood of black-swan events is that the experts who assess the likelihood of something happening usually find it very difficult to get any precise or compelling evidence about exactly how unlikely it is that something will happen in a specified time-period; and it is important to be very precise about the time-periods over which you are measuring probabilities when you are trying to get a sense of how worried the policy-makers should be about something. So, for example, if an event is described as having a 1 in 100,000 chance of occurring on any given *day* in the next ten years when it should actually have been described as having a 1 in 100,000 chance of occurring in any given *second* in the next ten years, then the chance of that event occurring at least once a decade rises to well above 99% (which sounds very worrying indeed).

So, when it comes to black-swan events, we need to understand fully the way that experts specify the risks and time-periods they are describing and be on guard against misunderstandings of what the experts are trying to tell us about the scale of those risks.

This is particularly true with events that could be triggered anywhere in an intricate global network. If the chance of a particular person at a particular address on a particular day causing a particular network event is only 1 in 100,000, and if there is no particular reason to suppose that the event is more or less likely to be triggered by someone else living at any other address anywhere else in the world on any other day, then the chance that this event will be caused by someone, at some address somewhere in the world at least once in a decade is also well over 99% – since there are literally billions of addresses in the world and lots of days in a decade. If this sounds implausible, just think about a national lottery: the chance of a particular person at a particular address winning the lottery today will be tiny; but the chance that someone, somewhere will win is 100%. So black-swan events are a lot more likely to occur in modern global networks, where the trigger-event can take place in any one of billions of highly specified locations, than it was in the old, much less interconnected world, where something happening in one very precisely defined place was not nearly as likely as it is today to have almost immediate and simultaneous effects in multitudes of other precisely defined places.

But the problem isn't just that the statistics are difficult for policy-makers to interpret correctly. When everything depends on the operation of hugely complex global networks, it is also easy for the experts to forget (or just not know) about some possible way for a particular black-swan event to be caused by someone somewhere in that network. These unknown unknowns are genuinely problematic – even in well-analysed areas. A classic case was the last banking crisis. When banking regulators modelled the risks for systemically important banks before the banking crisis, they looked at a wide range of scenarios. On the basis of their very thorough and expensive investigations, they concluded that the global banking system was robust in all of these scenarios. Unfortunately, they didn't include a scenario in which the entire wholesale inter-bank lending market dried up. It just didn't occur to them that this might happen, or that it might be triggered by relatively minor problems in one part of the global system gradually affecting the rest of the system. So they didn't look into what the effects would be if it did happen. We found out the answers only when it did happen – and then it turned out that these effects, as they ricocheted around the world, were catastrophic.

So black-swan events are not only more likely to happen in complex global networks, they are also more difficult to predict, because they are more likely to be caused by something that the forecasters haven't thought of.

In the end, this is the biggest problem of all, because – unlike the problems arising from the puzzling and often counter-intuitive nature of statistics and probabilities – it can't be cured just by applying time, effort and rationality. No amount of time or effort or rationality will guarantee that the experts will imagine the full range of possibilities. Indeed, in many ways it is the experts who are most likely to miss something about the future which, as a result of their intense understanding of the past, they naturally write off as 'impossible'. The more expert you become about operating in a particular system under normal circumstances, the more likely you are to take those normal circumstances for granted, and the less likely you are to speculate about what would happen if the circumstances were to be completely different from any that you have ever witnessed or heard about or read about. To the experts, the unprecedented can all too easily become the unimaginable.

In theory, policy-makers can overcome this tendency of experts to assume that the past is a guide to the future by bringing in 'free-thinkers' from outside the expert community. The aim, here, is to have the newcomers challenge the experts through 'thinking the unthinkable'. But such efforts often fail, because those who are engaged to 'think the unthinkable' either genuinely do just that – and end up being discounted by the experts as eccentric – or seek to preserve their standing with the experts by engaging in self-censorship in order to raise only those thoughts that the experts consider to be at least nearly thinkable. And even if one is lucky enough to find someone who has the remarkable combination of qualities required to convince the experts that he or she is not simply eccentric but has the ability to think outside the boxes constructed by the experts, there is no guarantee that this paragon-outsider will alight on the particular 'unthinkable' possibility that subsequently occurs. The outsider may be highly imaginative and highly plausible, but he or she is only human, and human beings do not have unlimited capacity to identify the range of the possible.

What is worse, if the outsiders (or indeed the experts themselves) do consider the possibility of the unimaginable coming to pass, they will naturally (a) attach a very low probability to it occurring and therefore (b) pay much less attention to it than they pay to the risks which they consider to be far more likely to materialize.

In principle, if something is very unlikely to occur but the consequences would be very, very bad if it did occur, then we should pay the same amount of attention to it that we would pay to something that would be much less bad but is much more likely to occur. If $p_1 \times q_1 = p_2 \times q_2$ (where p is the probability of the event occurring and q quantifies the amount of damage attached to the event if it does occur), then rationality dictates that we should worry exactly as much about event 1 (which has probability p_1 and causes damage q_1) as about event 2 (which has probability p_2 and causes damage q_2). But, in practice, this isn't the way the world works – because it isn't how our minds work. If you are told that there is a lion in the next room which has a 50% chance of breaking down the door and eating a member of your family in the next half hour, you are likely to be a whole lot more worried about this than about the fact that there is a 2% chance that all 25 members of your family will be killed by lightning in the next half hour due to very stormy conditions prevailing over your home. The lion seems an imminent and present danger, whereas the storm has a 98% chance of not happening. Odd, certainly – given that the damage done by the storm would be 25 times greater, just as the probability of it occurring is 25 times smaller. But this is just how we are programmed to think – perhaps partly because we inherit our genes from our distant ancestors who couldn't do very much about remote possibilities of major disasters but who might be able to take effective action against immediate, highly credible threats like lions in the next room (or the next cave).

The result is that, even when the statistics and probabilities have been correctly interpreted and the full range of the possible outcomes has been correctly established, policy-makers and business leaders have a strong tendency to concentrate more heavily on clear and present dangers than on remote eventualities, regardless of the quantity of damage that may arise from such remote eventualities. Enormous but very unlikely events just don't count for as much in business, media or government as large (but not nearly as large) events that are much more likely to occur. This is undoubtedly why it has proved so difficult over so many years to persuade people all over the world to take the more extreme and least probable risks associated with climate change as seriously as they should.

And this brings us to another problem about enormous, very unlikely events. They can sometimes seem *too enormous to be worth worrying about*. This is a strange phenomenon, which I shall call the 'then-we-will-all-be-dead syndrome' – because I have myself sat at meetings where some truly horrendous but very remote possibility is being contemplated, and someone at the meeting lightens the mood by saying 'oh, well we don't need to worry too much about that, since if that happens we will all be dead!', at which point everyone laughs and we go back to discussing clear and present dangers, where the scale is sufficiently small to be imaginable but the likelihood is high enough to cause concern. It's a bit like Parkinson's Law of Triviality that boards and committees have a tendency to focus on small items with which they can comfortably grapple rather than on much bigger items that seem to be beyond anything they can easily encompass.

For all of these reasons – the statistics that play games with our minds, the scope for misjudgements about units of measurement, the tendency to under-estimate network effects, the unknown unknowns that never get considered, the bias towards concern with the likely even when the unlikely should be more worrying, and the 'then-we-will-all-be-dead syndrome' – there is a systematic tendency in bureaucracies and businesses everywhere to underrate the significance of black-swan events.

The bad news is that this isn't just an academic issue. It is something that may have real consequences for real people. And it may affect real people by affecting real businesses.

The regulated businesses which operate the convergent networks at the centre of our economy are directly vulnerable to black-swan events of the sort illustrated in our story; their vulnerabilities to both natural hazards and human attacks pose important risks for our society.

But network failure doesn't just impact on such regulated businesses and their end-customers. It also affects a wide range of other businesses, many of which furnish goods and services that are part of the fabric of life as we know it.

There is a distressing tendency, both on the right and on the left of politics, and on the part of lazy journalists and commentators, to talk about the 'public services' as if they were the only businesses that perform important services for the public. On the right, this arises from a crude view of 'the market' as a jungle in which the fittest survive and in which the persistence of any normal business is a matter of indifference. On the left, it arises from the equally crude view that the motives and purposes of ordinary business have to do only with profit maximization and therefore leave the public interest wholly out of account. Both of these crude views miss the essential point that, while we can certainly tolerate some coming and going of particular firms over time, much of what we depend upon in order to go about our daily lives is in fact furnished by businesses that are *not* usually described as public services – and we would be very badly affected if they were all to shut down all at once, even for a short period.

Most fundamentally, there is the question of food. Manifestly, nothing could be more important for human survival. But, in advanced societies, few people have the means of home-producing substantial proportions of the food they need to survive; and, although most of us have ways of storing a certain amount of the food we purchase from retailers over a certain number of days, we are likely to run out after varying (often quite short) periods. Moreover, the most vulnerable – especially the very young, the very old and the very poor – are seriously exposed because of the specialized foods needed by babies, the aversion to waste exhibited by many of the frail elderly living alone, and the inability of the very poor to afford to keep large stocks. Accordingly, we all – and especially the most vulnerable among us – need to be able to buy food at regular intervals. Food outlets, from corner shops to hypermarkets and online retailers, and the whole intricate supply chains of producers, importers, processors, wholesalers and distributors that lie behind them, therefore constitute one of the most significant hidden 'public services'. The market failure of one of the retail outlets, or of a part of one supply chain, is of no great concern to the population at large; but a sudden and simultaneous closure of the whole food-supply system as a result of systemic failure, either in the retail outlets or in any one or more parts of the supply chain, would be of huge concern to enormous numbers of people.

Beyond the provision of food, there are other 'ordinary' businesses outside the regulated network sectors on which we rely far more than is commonly acknowledged.

The pharmacies provide a vivid example. At any given moment, almost all of those who need any given drug or medical aid either have a sufficient supply at home or can obtain spare supplies on an emergency basis from what is in most advanced countries a standard public service – namely, the health service. But no country has a health service that stocks sufficient drugs to provide rapid supply for the number of patients who would need them if there were a serious disruption in the normal supply through pharmacies. And, once again, it would be the very young and the very old (i.e. the most vulnerable) who would be most likely to depend on regular supplies of medicine and would therefore be most likely to suffer. So, as with the food retailers, the pharmacies (taken as a whole) constitute one of the hidden 'public services', despite the fact that they are not part of the publicly funded services or regulated networks (of public utilities such as energy, telecoms, etc.). And, as with food, there is a huge and complicated supply chain of pharmaceutical producers, importers, wholesalers and distributors lying behind the pharmacies themselves. Sustained and system-wide disruption of this supply chain would have a hugely detrimental impact on large numbers of vulnerable people across society as a whole.

Not all of the 'normal' non-network businesses that provide crucial public services are as obvious as food and pharmaceuticals. Some come into view only when things go very wrong. A classic example is the travel and holiday business. Most of the time, we rightly regard this as an optional extra – a treat that we all like to have available but which none of us needs to have at a particular moment. Who can reasonably say without irony that they 'simply have to have a holiday abroad'? And yet, this highly discretionary activity ceases to be so discretionary and becomes a matter of basic public service if you happen to be a traveller who has already gone abroad when the system breaks down. Having a holiday abroad on a given date is a bonus. Being on holiday abroad and not being able to get back home can be something else entirely. For some people under some circumstances, it may just be a monumental bore; but for other people under other circumstances, it can be a disaster. And here, too, it is more likely to be a disaster for the most vulnerable people than for those who are able-bodied and well-off.

For these reasons, the resilience a society needs in the face of network failure relates to a much wider range of businesses than just the network operators and what are usually regarded as basic, standard public services. We all have an interest in ensuring, so far as possible, that the goods and services on which we rely will continue to be available, or at least that some reasonable proxies for them will continue to be available, if the businesses that normally provide them are prevented from doing so over a sustained period as a result of prolonged and systemic network failure, regardless of whether that is caused by natural hazards or human interventions.

We shouldn't, however, restrict ourselves to worrying only about the businesses that fall into this category. A large number of firms in other sectors, whose interruption over a period of days would not particularly matter to the public as a whole and which cannot therefore be described as hidden public services, are nevertheless of great concern to the people that own them, run them and work for them, and of course for particular customers. To take an example, the participants in the vast production and supply system for automobiles cannot be regarded as a form of immediately necessary public service: we can all quite happily wait a little longer for a new car. But for some of these businesses themselves – those who invest in them, work in them and use their products – a sustained interruption of activity due to network failure can have crippling, long-term consequences. In an industry whose whole mode of production depends on 'just in time' working, a supplier in country X who fails to provide a key component on the day required because of interruption due to network failure in country X may well find that the manufacturers in countries Y and Z, who were his customers, cease to be his customers thereafter, bringing his business to an abrupt and permanent halt.

So there is not only good reason for society and the state to be concerned about the resilience of a wide range of businesses in the face of sustained network failure; there is also good reason for many businesses to be concerned about this same thing in the interest of their own commercial survival.

The next question, of course, is how far different kinds of business are really dependent on the convergent networks and are hence exposed to serious risks in the event of a sustained network failure. It is probably true that all modern businesses in advanced economies use a range of modern networks (at the very least electricity and telecommunications) to some extent. But of course there is a great difference between using a network under normal circumstances and being dependent upon the sustained availability of that network either for your own commercial survival, or in order to provide a crucial (albeit possibly hidden) public service, or both. And many businesses are in the lucky position of having what one might call 'natural fallback options'.

The simplest fallback option is just to close down for the time that the networks are unavailable. This is a thoroughly feasible solution for businesses whose long-term customer relationships are unaffected by a period of closure, whose services are not essential to the community they serve, and whose financial condition will not be seriously impaired in the long term by a period without revenue.

The next simplest fallback is to run the business

during the time of network failure without having recourse to the networks that have failed. This, too, may be thoroughly feasible, even for businesses that (in a cashless society, for example) are wholly dependent on the networks under normal circumstances – if the nature of their business is such that they can find a temporary, non-network way of carrying on (e.g. by offering their cashless customers some form of paper-based credit for a short period).

There are, in fact, many thousands of businesses in any advanced economy that will have both of these very simple options open to them in the event of network failure. Take the example of a rural riding school and equestrian centre. A five-day disruption of all the key networks of the kind illustrated in my parable would obviously be a significant nuisance for such an enterprise. But a nuisance is not the same thing as a catastrophe. If the enterprise simply closed down for the five days, it would probably be able to keep the horses alive and fed on the basis of the stocks it normally carries; its staff would probably be sufficiently local to be able to continue at least this level of activity even in the event of systemic network failure; and its customers would be very unlikely to take their custom elsewhere after the disruption merely because of the closure. Nor would any members of the community lack for some necessity as a result of the enterprise being closed for such a length of time. If, on the other hand, there were enough customers and enough of the staff near enough at hand to continue operating during the period of network failure (as there might well be in a rural area), then keeping the enterprise going during the period of disruption might also be feasible, at least during daylight hours, not least because of the regularities that make arrangements by telecommunications unnecessary for many such businesses, and the fact that regular customers could be trusted with paper-based credit transactions in an emergency.

The important point about examples like this is that they bring out the need for a balanced appreciation of the risks that we are dealing with here. Unlike nuclear Armageddon or the Earth being struck by a massive meteorite, the failure of convergent networks that may well be caused in our generation, either by natural or by human agency, is emphatically *not* an 'all bets are off' scenario. This is part of the problem that we are bound to encounter in persuading important and busy people to take network failure as seriously as it deserves. As Hannah Arendt said so powerfully about a much worse set of events, it is the banality of the evil that is so disturbing: life will carry on through a period of network failure; much will go on operating more or less as it did before, with some necessary adjustment; other things will close temporarily, with relatively little long-term adverse effect. So there is the temptation to conclude, falsely, that the whole of life will continue without much adverse effect. In fact, the effects on some people may be horrific if appropriate fallback mechanisms are not available. And the same is true in relation to 'normal' non-network-operating businesses. Some of them will suffer little, if at all. But many others will be far more vulnerable. And in a subset of those businesses that are vulnerable, their vulnerability will ripple outwards into the lives of large numbers of vulnerable people for whom they normally provide critical (even if hidden) public services.

4

OUT IN THE DARKNESS

Out in the darkness, Bill Donoghue knew quite enough about the workings of government to be able to imagine the sorts of conversation that must be going on in COBR. But he had too much on his mind to spend time thinking about the problems likely to be exercising the PM and other ministers. The main issue for him was staying awake. It was a long while since he had tried driving anywhere in the early hours, and he found that doing so at the age of 50 was a rather different experience. Besides, he was wholly out of practice because – as he now realized – he had become completely used to letting the car drive him on long trips. After a frenzy of turnings and turnings-back, he had at last found his way to the A30, and was now well advanced along the 'longest lane in England'. So there was no longer a problem about finding the way. But just keeping alert, and actually driving the car at this time of night, particularly in these freezing conditions, was proving to be much more difficult than he had imagined.

It was a huge relief when he finally saw the sign indicating that he was entering Sherborne. Just a short hop through the town and on to Yeovil, then he could head for the hospital to see Elaine before carrying on to her mother in East Coker.

The car park, when he arrived at the hospital, was much fuller than he had expected. And he was surprised by the number of ambulances that seemed to be queued up on the ramp up to A&E and on the street outside; they stretched so far down the road that one of them was practically blocking the unlit visitors' entrance. But this was nothing compared with the scene that greeted him as he entered reception. It was just before 4.30 a.m. on New Year's Day, and Bill had expected to find the reception area nearly deserted – instead of which it appeared that half the population of Yeovil had descended on the hospital. They all seemed to be heading, as he was, towards the A&E department, with the usual assortment of minor ailments visible in many cases. It occurred to him that New Year's Eve revels would presumably have been responsible for much of this; so perhaps the Health Secretary had been right to insist on consultants like Elaine being present at this ungodly hour. But he also caught two snatches of conversation that proved the fixed-line phone system wasn't working here any more than it was in London, and his own repeated failures to get any signal from his mobile on the way down to Somerset had already persuaded him that the mobile networks were down; so presumably no one could reach 111 to be 'triaged' into the recently established 24-hour health centres by phone – and many of them had clearly come to the hospital instead.

It didn't take him more than a few seconds to spot Elaine once he got into the A&E area. She was talking to three other members of the medical staff, who looked as worn out as she did. Clearly, this was not a moment for a long conversation. That would come later, perhaps much later. He made his way over, attracted her attention and explained to her briefly that he was on his way to see her mother, adding that he had plenty of battery life in the car and that he would come back to the hospital once he had satisfied himself that all was well with Mary. She darted him a look of thanks, squeezed his arm in her usual fashion and turned back to the discussion with her colleagues.

As he came back out to reception, he asked the woman at the desk why there were so many ambulances queued up outside. 'Oh, it has been a nightmare. All the ambulances that were here or on their way here when we went over to reserve generation have had to remain here because they have lost contact with their control centre and don't know where they are needed.'

Of course. Why hadn't he thought of that? Whatever

had gone wrong with the communications systems had gone wrong with *all* of the communications systems – including the ambulances, and therefore presumably also the police and fire service. He hoped to goodness that someone was busy putting all this right.

The drive to East Coker took him only ten minutes. He parked outside Mary's thatched cottage on Back Lane – just a stone's throw from St Michael and All Angels, the fine old Somerset church immortalized by T. S. Eliot in one of his *Four Quartets* and where his remains lie buried. Unsurprisingly, at just after 5 a.m. on New Year's Day, the cottage was in darkness and there was no sign of life. Luckily, he had Mary's spare key in his coat, having put it there when driving her home after Boxing Day. He let himself in as quietly as he could and tiptoed up the steep staircase on the other side of the hallway. As he could hear Mary snoring gently in her bedroom, he decided that he would set his alarm for 8 a.m. (that part of his smartphone seemed to be operating fine) and creep into the spare room for three hours of much-needed sleep. The room was appreciably colder than he would have liked, but by piling the spare blankets that Mary kept in the wardrobe on top of the bed, he was able to create a cocoon sufficiently warm to enable him to sleep. Perhaps by sunrise someone would have put the nation's technology back together again, and this whole episode would be a thing of the past.

The alarm, when it sounded, seemed part of a horribly confused dream in which the Governor's parlour of the Bank of England had somehow become an ambulance depot. But it took him only a few seconds to reorient himself and to see the reassuring sight of the trees in Mary's garden out of the window of the spare room. The sun was rising across the valley on what promised to be a fine day, but the room was horribly cold.

There was no hot water emanating from the taps in the bath, so he restricted his ablutions to a rapid dash of ice-cold water on his face. Once rudimentarily 'washed' and dressed, he made his way along the upper landing to Mary's room. Like many people of her age, she tended to get up late in the morning – often, as he gathered, after a rather wakeful night. Sure enough, she was still sleeping. So he went down to the kitchen to make toast and coffee. The discovery – obvious, when one thought about it – that neither the toaster nor the electric kettle were operating reminded him, if he needed any reminding in the cold house, of the fact that whatever had caused last night's nightmare was still disrupting normal life.

Unfazed, he cut a slice from the loaf in the bread-bin and launched into a breakfast of bread and water. At least the water was clearly working – though he did briefly wonder how long that would last.

The worst of it was that he had absolutely no news to guide him. On New Year's Day, one wouldn't have expected any newspapers – not that there were many of those left nowadays. Obviously, he couldn't use his smartphone for online news. The digital radio, which was battery powered, just displayed 'no signal' when he turned it on. And there was no more joy than he expected from either the television or the fixed phone line. His thoughts turned to Mary. How long was all of this going to last? And how was he going to arrange for her to be properly looked after in time to enable him to get back to the Bank of England before the Eastern markets began to wake up?

He heard sounds of stirring above him, and went back up to her room, announcing himself gently as he reached her landing. 'Hello, Mary. It's me. There seems to have been a rather major power cut that has cut off all communications, and your heating. So I thought I should come to see how you are.'

'Thank you, dear. It's good of you to have come. But I'm sure I shall be fine. The nice woman who comes to help me with dressing and breakfast should be here any moment.'

He knew better than to argue with this. Mary wouldn't want her routine disrupted.

'Fine. I'll wait downstairs until she comes. There are plenty of good books to read in your sitting-room.'

Half an hour later. No sign of the carer. And, of course, there was no point in trying to find out from Mary whom he could ring to enquire about what was happening.

He went upstairs again and, with slight difficulty, persuaded her to let him help her dress, before assisting her down to the kitchen for some rudimentary breakfast. So far, so good. But what was he to do now? As he couldn't make a phone call, there was no way of finding out whether the carer would be coming at all. He would have to wait at least until tomorrow before finding anybody in the local bureaucracy who would be able to help. But, as the officer who had volunteered for New Year's duty, he couldn't just leave the Bank exposed until then.

He decided that this was something he definitely needed to discuss with Elaine. Automatically, he reached for his smartphone, before realizing that this was futile. He would have to go back into Yeovil.

▲

A meeting had been arranged for 10 a.m. in the COBR suite at the Cabinet Office, to give time for the Civil Contingencies Secretariat to produce a list of attendees. Based on the Cabinet Office list, the army, using their independent comms and fossil-fuel transport, had done an excellent job of collecting the relevant people from the ministries, firms, agencies and public services responsible for the key services. So the internal sound-proofed room was now full of people. But there was little of the camaraderie that usually lightened the atmosphere at these meetings. Everyone present was too aware of the scale of the difficulties they were facing.

Jan Sikorski, who was showing every sign of a night spent working rather than sleeping, opened: 'Prime Minister, we now have just about everyone relevant round the table. I wonder whether you would like me to begin by summarizing briefly the current situation, as we haven't yet been able to prepare a report of common recognized information – which we will be doing at six-hourly intervals from mid-day today?'

The PM, with remarkable sangfroid, had used the previous few hours to catch a night's sleep before travelling in from Chequers and was clearly wide awake:

'Yes, Jan. That would be extremely helpful.'

'Thank you, Prime Minister. The situation, so far as we currently know it, is as follows:

'As you and your colleagues agreed during the late-night COBR call, there appears to have been a severe space-weather event at just before midnight last night. National Grid, who are here this morning, have confirmed that the grid as a whole failed at about that time. They are now working at gradual restoration. But they are severely hampered by poor communications, because all normal comms systems appear to have been disrupted either by the grid failure or by the space weather itself or both. As we heard last night, they, like the armed forces, are functioning on the basis of old-fashioned walkie-talkie communications. We estimate that it will take at least five days for the grid to be fully restored, though there will be patches of power coming on and off in various parts of the country as power stations are brought on and the system begins to be balanced from lunchtime today onwards. National Grid anticipate that some transformers and other critical items will have been damaged by the magnetic pulse. We expect to receive a clearer picture of such damage to grid equipment in the course of the day.

'You and other participants are already aware that the armed forces have capabilities that enable them to operate despite the problems in the civilian systems. You may want to ask the Defence Secretary for his assessment. We understand that the Chief of the Defence Staff has been in touch with the Health Secretary and has, at the Health Secretary's request, despatched teams to investigate and report on conditions in all major hospitals. We should have reports from that exercise by mid-afternoon. Our expectation is that reserve generators at most hospitals will last for something like the five days that it takes to bring the power back online.

'We have the chief executive of Ofcom here; you may want to ask her for a view on the prospects for communications systems over the next few days. Our understanding is that neither national nor international comms are likely to be restored until the grid is fully functional.

'We also have the Local Government Secretary present. You might want to ask him for a view on the adult social care system under these circumstances. I should emphasize the importance of this issue, given that – as established at the earlier COBR call – we are clear that household heating systems will be out of service across the country, and frail, elderly people will not be able to call for help.

'In this context, the weather is obviously highly relevant. I gather that many of the Met Office systems have failed. But they are still able to offer predictions based on trend analysis. You may want to ask for their observations on likely developments over the next few days.

'Finally, we are concerned about the fact that, from tomorrow onwards, when the shops would normally be open, it will be impossible for customers to make even essential purchases due to the total failure of credit card systems. The duty officer at the Bank of England has apparently left the building and cannot be traced; but the Chancellor of the Exchequer has commissioned work from senior Treasury officials who have been contacted via the army, and she will be able to brief you on the next steps.'

None of this gave the PM much comfort. Despite the orderly, bureaucratic management of the meeting proposed by CCS, he had the strong impression – reading between the lines – that the collective state of knowledge had not advanced much since the middle of the night, and there was, as yet, no sign of any plan to deal with the social care crisis. But he knew from many previous COBR meetings that the best bet was to follow roughly the order of enquiry suggested by CCS before attempting to formulate a plan of action.

'Right. I think we can take it as read that National Grid will be doing everything it can to get the power system up and running again, and we discussed the timescales for that last night. So let's start, as you suggest, with the military. Defence Secretary: what can you tell us?'

Like Jan Sikorski, and unlike the PM, Harold Stuart had clearly spent the night awake – presumably in discussions with the military. But he was still relatively upbeat.

'As Jan says, Prime Minister, the army has been very active over the last few hours. I want to pay tribute to the huge efforts that have been made. I should begin by saying that the UK remains protected. The nuclear deterrent remains fully operational. The Royal Air Force Quick Reaction Alert is also operating normally. So far as the land army is concerned, we are operating on the basis of pyramid communications, as planned for such eventualities, with information and commands being passed up and down the pyramid. The consciously primitive resilient comms equipment does not allow direct communication among teams at the base of the pyramid. We will produce a report on the hospital generators for the Health

Secretary before this evening's COBR. My main concern now is to know whether you want me to concentrate on providing a parallel military comms network for adult social care, or on helping to open up supplies of food and other essentials from supermarkets, or on supporting the ambulance, police and fire services – all of which appear to have been effectively demobilized by the lack of communications and all of which are likely soon to run out of electric charge for their vehicles. I will need a clear mandate, expressed in the form of a request for military assistance from the civil powers, in order to direct my 30,000-plus active UK-based service personnel where you feel they are most needed.'

'Thank you, Harold. We will certainly aim to give you that by the end of this meeting. But I'd like next to hear from the Met Office, so that we all know what conditions we should expect over the next three or four days.'

The Met Office's report – in traditional style – was hedged and qualified. But the gist was plain. If the trends established before the monitoring systems all went blank were to continue, the sky would remain clear (so no floods or snowfall) but Britain would be in for some of the coldest weather it had experienced in recent times.

The PM was not surprised to hear this. Stepping out of Chequers at breakfast time had been enough to lead him to suppose that they were in for a cold snap. This brought the question of the frail elderly into high relief. Most of the population could probably withstand a few days of cold and short rations. Many of those who were old and frail could not. He needed to ensure that they were somehow brought to somewhere warm, and that they were somehow fed. But how?

'Let's turn to you, Eric. How do we get the first-tier local authorities to keep their adult services going under these circumstances? And how can the military best help to make that happen?'

Sir Eric Bullient had been brought out of deep retirement on the parliamentary backbenches to take the helm at the Ministry of Housing, Communities and Local Government when unfortunate events had precipitated the departure of his immediate predecessor. He was now in his seventh year of his second tour of duty at the department – and, in addition to his famed bonhomie, he had enormous experience. But he was by no means as confident as the PM hoped he might be.

'Well, Prime Minister, that is indeed the sixty-four-thousand-dollar-question. To which, at this precise moment, I admit freely I don't know the answer.

'I think we can assume that the residential homes will somehow be able to "make do and mend" for four or five days. Clearly, the biggest challenge is in domiciliary care. We have around three-quarters of a million domiciliary care workers providing care at home for about 1.25 million elderly people. In general, each care worker will have a rota, and I would expect most of them to continue to follow that rota in the absence of any instructions to the contrary – at least for the next few days, during which they will presumably see the signs that someone is trying to get the system back to normal.

'I anticipate three major problems. First, even assuming that most of them have fully charged cars this morning, many – especially in rural areas – are likely to run out of battery power well before five days are up; second, if they find an elderly person in difficulty on one of their rounds, whether because of the cold or otherwise, they will not be able to reach either 111 or the emergency services because they will have no functioning communications systems; and third, many of them are going to find it difficult to help produce meals for their clients if no food can be bought and no cooking of any kind can be done.

'I do not currently have a solution to any of these problems.'

At least, that was honest. But it wasn't enough – because the PM had to get some handle on the scale of the challenge before he could make any decisions about where to direct his scant resources.

'Thanks, Eric, for that candid assessment. Can you tell us what you estimate as the effect if we can't solve any of those problems before the energy and communications systems come back into operation?'

Bullient had clearly been thinking about this question himself.

'Well, Prime Minister, I can offer you only a completely amateur guess. If we assume that domiciliary care, at least for the two-thirds of elderly people that live outside city centres, will cease after, say, two days, and if we assume that half of these elderly people will not have the capacity (either by themselves or with help from neighbours, family or friends) to keep themselves warm without any heating or to prepare food for themselves, then we might be facing severe medical repercussions for as many as 400,000 people. I have no means of guessing what proportion of those elderly people will either die or become terminally ill within the five-day period – but I think we should not be surprised if this, too, applied in half the cases: so perhaps 200,000 fatalities. That would clearly represent, by some orders of magnitude, the largest civilian catastrophe in this country since the pandemic flu after the First World War.'

There was actually nothing surprising about what Eric Bullient had said. Anyone in the room could have done the same simple maths, and would have come to similar conclusions. Of course, the number was pure conjecture. It could be half as large or twice as large. But they were clearly dealing with something that, in the absence of a solution, was going to result not in tens or hundreds, or even in thousands or tens of thousands, but in hundreds of thousands of deaths.

His words hung in the air. The Prime Minster, whose mouth had suddenly become very dry, swallowed and cleared his throat.

'Given that sobering thought, let's hear from Ofcom. Sheila, is there any chance of restoring any serious communications, beyond the prehistoric military and grid walkie-talkies, while we wait for the grid to restore power?'

Professor Dame Sheila Hart, after a lifetime spent as a regulatory economist in Oxford, was not given to lengthy speeches. Nor was she in any doubt. By the time she had arrived in her current post a year back, all the decisions about 6G, 7G and the fibre networks had long since been taken, and it had been made abundantly clear to her by GCHQ and by her own staff that the whole communications, banking, transport and energy infrastructure of the country would go down if the National Grid went down. Her task now was to ensure that no one wasted time or effort pursuing phantasmagoric solutions.

'I'm afraid not, Prime Minister. The construction of the Internet and of package-switched communication is such that, even if we had stand-alone power supplies for some parts of the systems we have in place, the amount of data seeking routes through the network would cause collapse. This is because each package of data seeks a new route if the most obvious route is blocked. So, when a large part of the network falls over, the amount of traffic leaps upwards. It's as if you blocked half the streets in London; all the cars would be doubling back all over the place, causing much more than twice the usual traffic. Recognizing this intrinsic feature of modern IP-based communications, we did have, back in the early 2020s, an arrangement enabling basic GSM texts to be sent and received over the main 4G transmitters and the back-haul fibre system powered by stand-alone generation. But, once we moved to UAV-based 5G coverage, we decided that the additional cost of sustaining that basic texting system was disproportionate, given the extremely low probability of a National Grid failure. So we now have no mass communication system that can operate without the grid.'

At this point, Jane Baldwin, who had been reluctant to interrupt the PM's handling of the meeting, intervened: 'I take it, Sheila, that this implies that all domestic purchase transactions and all normal communication – including financial data flows – with the rest of the world will be out of action for the next five days?'

'I'm afraid so, Chancellor. The cashless economy is rendered non-existent when there are no electronic financial flows. And our normal external comms are just as IP-dependent as our domestic communications. I should also say something about broadcasting. Clearly, there will be no reception for TVs that depend on mains power or for those who receive broadcasts via the net (now a great majority). In theory, battery-powered digital radios could still receive. But they will not be able to obtain UK broadcasts because, although the major UK broadcasters do have considerable back-up power sources, they now use IP-based systems to connect their broadcast centres with their transmitters. This was a resilience issue raised by CCS and the Minister for the Cabinet Office. But it was decided that the efficiencies generated by a move to the net for these communications would outweigh any decrease in resilience. And the local commercial broad-casters, who have direct, old-fashioned comms with their transmitters, unfortunately don't have any back-up gen-eration. We contemplated stipulating such back-up in the recent licensing round, but concluded that it would not be affordable. So I'm afraid the short version is that there will be no broadcasting at all until the grid is back up, and no major national broadcasting until the Internet is also functioning again.'

The PM sensed that, if he wasn't careful, they would all spend the next half-hour charting the scale of the problem rather than devising a solution to the crisis in care of the elderly – which was clearly by far the most serious imme-diate consequence of their immediate predicament.

'I think, Jane, we can take it as established fact that both the normal electronic-money economy and our normal international communications will take some days to restore. But almost all of our population will, one way or another, work out how to deal with that. The challenge we have to meet is the prospect of severe problems among the frail elderly. Until we have a plan to prevent that happening, we should focus on nothing else. I want to go back to the army. Let me put this to you, CDS: if the Defence Secretary and I were to ask you to concentrate exclusively on helping the frail elderly to survive for the next five days, what plan could you give us?'

The Chief of the Defence Staff had been dreading this moment. He was very keenly aware that this was the sort of operation which would have required months of planning, trials and documentation before being put into action. And he was also very keenly aware that no such preparations had been made. The events they were now witnessing had been seen as too remote an eventuality to make sense of expending time and effort on plans of this sort. But, somehow, the army was going to have to try to come up with an answer. So he had better make that sound as convincing as he could, and then try to translate his own glossy rhetoric into something as good as could be done in the twenty-four or forty-eight hours available. But, at the same time, he needed to give the PM and others some real sense of the dimensions of the task.

'Well, Prime Minister, with about 30,000 troops immediately available, we can't possibly hope to have the army reach out directly to any noticeable proportion of the 1.25 million frail, elderly people living in their own homes. So we are going to have to lever the use of our troops, by employing our comms and logistics to establish an effective command and control system for the 0.75 million domiciliary care workers. We will also need to find some means of creating warm spaces in each area of the country, and of stocking those spaces with food and other provisions, so that we can use the command and control system to organize lifts into the warm spaces for whichever of the frail, elderly people are identified by the domiciliary care workers as needing such support. At present, I can't tell COBR much more than that. But I hope to have at least the outline of a more detailed plan within the next twelve hours, which could be further refined overnight, brought back to COBR for approval tomorrow morning, and then put immediately into action. We will need to start by working with the Communities Secretary and the Health Secretary to find out how we can make contact with the local authorities and agencies that employ the domiciliary care workers – and then work out how, through the employers, we can make contact with the care workers themselves.'

The PM had chaired quite enough COBR meetings to know how to translate this seemingly smooth presentation of the military 'plan'. It was clear that there was no plan. The Chief of the Defence Staff didn't even know how his troops would be able to make contact with 750,000 care workers – much less what they would do once the contact had been made. But this was not the time for recriminations. He would just have to hope that the military, with their remarkable ability to think and act fast, would be able to think and act fast enough.

5

FRAGILITY AND RESILIENCE

The point of our story, and of the argument so far, is that our economy and society are becoming increasingly dependent on a web of interconnected global networks, and that this increasingly exposes us to the risk of everything being brought crashing down by someone's actions or some force of nature that we hadn't thought likely, or even possible.

The problem is that this increasing risk of an unexpected meltdown is built into the technologies on which we all now depend. Every time the Internet-based and electronically based networks take a step forward towards convergence (through the Internet of Things, demand-responsive smart grids, autonomous electric vehicles, and so forth), the potential gains increase, but so does the risk of universal, simultaneous meltdown. The risk isn't a by-product of connectedness; it is an intrinsic part of connectedness – because connectivity connects individual risks into a system of risk.

Of course, it would in theory be possible for us to get off this line of technological evolution. We could – in some fantasy world – collectively decide to un-digitize all of the basic activities in our economy and society; we could decide to remove all the links between our computers and the Internet; we could decide not to communicate via tablets and smartphones; we could decide not to drive electric and autonomous vehicles; we could decide not to use electricity and electronic devices to control just about everything in our homes and businesses, public services and government departments; we could decide to go back to snail-mail, cheques and cash as the way of buying things. In fact, there is no limit to the amount of techno-logical regress that we could mandate for ourselves if we wished to do so.

But one has only to list these possibilities to see how ludicrous an idea this is. The sacrifices that it would entail are gargantuan.

If one country unilaterally took action on all of these fronts and became the only place in which people didn't use electricity, electronics and the Internet-based commu-nications and control systems now increasingly available, this would have colossal economic impacts. The country in question would lose all the increases in productivity and reductions in cost that these modern, convergent technologies have brought to our service and manufacturing industries. To remain competitive with the other economies that maintained all of these efficiency gains, the population would have to pay itself a fraction of what it now pays itself to create sufficient reductions in labour costs to offset the losses in the productivity of labour. A rich, technologically sophisticated country which adopted such a policy would head towards being, if not a low-income economy, at best a middle-income country of the kind now to be found in some parts of Latin America and Asia. And the policy is no more imaginable for poorer countries – because, although they have less technology to lose, they start from a lower base of labour costs, and would have to make poorer populations still poorer. In short, it is wildly implausible that any country would unilaterally opt for such technological regress, regardless of their development.

Of course, if – pretty unimaginably – the whole world could be persuaded to abandon all of these technologies simultaneously and to put a block on technological progress thereafter (via a Strategic Technology Reduction Treaty), then each country following this regressive path wouldn't be returning to the past on its own and therefore wouldn't be at a huge competitive disadvantage compared with economies based on convergent technologies. So no country would necessarily become *relatively* poorer. But, even if such a fantasy-treaty could be made real, the whole world would lose vast numbers of advantages. Everyone would be absolutely poorer. Humanity wouldn't, collectively, be able to produce anything like as many goods and services as we make today – let alone as many as we will be able to produce tomorrow if we maintain technological progress. It would be a question of undoing most of the last forty years of growth, and then prohibiting ourselves from growing at the current rate for the foreseeable future. For people in high-income countries, the immediate effect would be to return to something like the standard of living experienced in the mid-1970s; that would be bad enough. But for the emerging economies of the East, and even more for the poor nations of the South, this would be unimaginably serious. The consequences, not just in terms of quality of life but also in terms of stability, would be very difficult to deal with.

While we are at it, the ecological and social effects of any such global decision to regress technologically would be at least as great as the economic effects. Although we might use rather less energy if our economies reverted to a less network-dependent form, our ability to produce and use energy efficiently – through smart grids, smart meters, dynamic response, electric transport and all the rest of it – would be hugely reduced, making it vastly more difficult to limit carbon emissions. Our ability to predict and respond to climatic and weather-induced conditions such as flooding would be drastically affected. Even quite simple things like more efficient use of water to slow down the water cycle and the reduction of air pollution would become much more cumbersome and expensive, and hence much less likely to happen – with severe ecological impacts. Meanwhile, the social effects would be to reduce the effectiveness of health and social care, to impede all sorts of distance learning, and to increase costs of the vast range of goods and products whose prices have been significantly reduced by the Internet and its associated technologies. So, as is usually the case with reactionary and regressive policies, it would be the environment, the poor and the just-about-managing sections of the global population who would suffer most.

One way and another, the short answer to the question 'can we go backwards and undo the technological progress of the last forty years?' is for all practical purposes 'NO'. That is presumably why, as far as I am aware, no serious and widely based political grouping is putting forward a programme of this kind anywhere in the world. There are small groups on the fringe who may at least dally with such ideas – for example, some of the most extreme eco-warriors. But there is no sign of them obtaining any serious traction.

The fact that we can't in practice halt and reverse the evolution of the convergent technologies means that we are inevitably heading towards an array of risks that imperil us. People who have been enriched and enabled by the new networks may not realize that the enriched world, as they encounter it, is now more fragile than it once was, because it is prone to sudden, wide-area failures to which our ancestors, with their simpler and poorer world, were much less exposed. But, whether realized by the population as a whole, the exposure is real. And this inevitably tempts policy-makers into searching for a guaranteed defence against such wide-area failures.

This approach can be described as the *resilience strategy*. It has many adherents in governments around the world. Almost every rich and middle-income country in both the East and West has now begun to develop increasingly sophisticated mechanisms for defending itself against a wide range of natural and human attacks on its critical national infrastructure. And even the poorer countries with less-developed infrastructures are taking a heightened interest. There are innumerable international gatherings to discuss cyber-security, defence against the flooding caused by climate change, and other related issues. The results are in many respects impressive.*

---

* To take the UK as an example, in recent years there has been: a massive increase in public spending on cyber-defence; an equal (and largely successful) effort to persuade private-sector businesses that they should invest in improving their resilience to cyber-attack; the creation of a new National Cyber Centre that will bring these two strands of activity together; vastly increased public-sector investment in flood defence; the establishment of a new reinsurance scheme that contains strong incentives for vulnerable householders to defend their

But, despite all of the impressive and desirable progress that is being made in implementing resilience strategies around the world, there is a real deficiency in this whole approach. The deficiency is that no system of defence can ever be complete. One can construct more and more elaborate walls to keep out more and more types of invasion. But one can never be sure that one has predicted all possible types of natural and human invader; and one can never be sure that the walls will prove to be robust in the face of all the weapons at the disposal of the invaders. With the speed of technological progress, the extent of the ingenuity and diversity of the categories of human antagonists, as well as the scale and complexity of the potential threats from natural geo-physical and space phenomena to the global networks on which we increasingly depend, it is likely that a gap in the defences will, at some point, be revealed. The extent of the damage caused by a successful invasion through that gap is likely to be large, because of the very same

---

properties more effectively against flooding; new approaches to river catchment management to reduce the chance of fluvial flooding; reinforcement of the grids and distribution systems for electricity, gas and water; serious efforts to diminish the danger of key infrastructure being affected by space weather; the establishment of a much more highly organized national risk register, and new measures to reduce the likelihood of each identified critical risk on that risk register. Similar patterns of activity to reinforce defences and to reduce risks are to be found in many other jurisdictions.

interconnectedness that makes the global networks so useful to us the rest of the time.

One possible reaction to this fact of incomplete defence – indeed, the reaction that mainly prevails in governmental circles around the world today – is to divert yet more intellectual and practical effort into identifying potential forms of invasion, and into strengthening yet further the walls around our critical infrastructure. This is a worthy endeavour, and we should certainly welcome the fact that governments are increasingly giving greater priority to such efforts at improved network defence. But there is nevertheless a distinctly Sisyphean air to the project. No sooner is another effort made than another potential threat emerges. The stone keeps on rolling back down the hill.

An alternative approach is proposed by Nassim Taleb, one of the most interesting thinkers currently writing in this field. Taleb has a fully developed thesis about black-swan events and about how we should respond to them, based on what he describes as *anti-fragility*.

The starting point of the anti-fragility strategy is that, just as bad black-swan events can have catastrophic effects on fragile systems, good black-swan events can have transformative effects for the better if systems are designed in such a way as to benefit from the innovations that such events prompt (making them anti-fragile). What is meant, here, by a 'good' black-swan event is emphatically not just a large collection of manna from heaven – but rather a highly challenging event that prompts an anti-fragile system to rethink and innovate. Taleb's point is that well-constructed systems (e.g. market economies) contain the capacity to respond through innovation when they come under serious and successful attack, whereas ill-designed systems (e.g. command economies) cannot respond in this way, because they are constructed solely to repel invaders rather than to learn from invasions. Taleb amplifies this thesis in various interesting ways (suggesting, for example, that teleological, top-down structures are likely to be far more fragile and far less anti-fragile than structures within which individuals can take the risk of 'tinkering' incrementally, searching for unpredictable gains through trial and error). But the central hypothesis – that intelligently 'anti-fragile' networks can improve through innovative response to attacks – is the item that matters in the context of network vulnerability.

We need to ask whether, instead of focusing on (or solely focusing on) defence, those responsible for our critical national infrastructure should aim at making it anti-fragile – in other words, capable of improving through learning from attack? There seem to be two clear answers to this question, depending on the time-scales.

In the long term, we surely do want the networks at the core of our infrastructure to have the capacity to learn from attack. It is true, as Taleb argues, that participants in open-textured systems like free markets will tend to respond to misadventures by innovating – and it is in part this capacity for incremental innovation by people in the face of adversity that gives such free market systems the extraordinary power as engines of long-term prosperity that they have demonstrated throughout human history. Likewise, Taleb is convincing when he points to the fact that this quality of rebound is evidently and disastrously lacking in unwieldy, top-down command systems, which can sometimes achieve spectacular advances for a short period, but which fall under their own weight in the long run. Moreover, with the rise of artificial intelligence, this same capacity for intelligent, innovative response to crisis may well become a more and more prevalent feature of global networks. It is, after all, the hallmark of artificial intelligence that it involves machines learning from experience in somewhat the same way as human beings.

But, in the short term, the impact of successful black-swan attacks on critical infrastructure and the consequent impact on the life (and death) of citizens and businesses is much too great for us to content ourselves with the thought that, in the long run, the experience may prove educative. This is the whole point of the story told in this book about what might happen on New Year's Eve 2037. It is one thing to say, when the storm has abated, that it

will usefully have tested our defences, and that participants (and maybe, in due course, the electronic networks
themselves) will be jolted into improvements which we
would not otherwise have imagined possible; it is quite
another to say in the midst of the storm that the mangled
bodies are a price worth paying. The immediate disaster is
simply too great to be treated solely as a useful source of
learning. In response to any such immediate attack, both
government on behalf of society and the business community need an immediate response that will rapidly and
successfully provide some means of lessening the impact
of the disaster itself. Only then can we hope to tolerate it
sufficiently at the time to begin to be able to appreciate
the potential long-term benefits arising from innovative
responses.

Given that preventative defence strategies cannot
provide perfect protection of key networks, and that
anti-fragility strategies leave us exposed to unacceptable short-term effects of network failure, we clearly
need a 'third way'. This 'third way' does not consist in
strengthening existing defences. Nor does it consist in
tolerating short-term disasters in the hope of long-term
gain. Instead, it consists in consciously building fallback
options that will enable us to carry on during a period
when the key networks have failed.

Like anti-fragility strategies, the *fallback-option strategy*
admits the possibility (even the likelihood) that the walls

defending key networks will be breached by black-swan events of unpredictable kinds. Like preventative defence strategies, the fallback-option strategy recognizes that, whatever the long-run effects of such breaches, the short-term effects may be unacceptably bad. But, at the same time, it acknowledges that the gains for humanity in normal peacetime conditions from such networks are so great that we will want to continue to depend on them even if they are exposed to unacceptable short-term risks and cannot be perfectly inoculated against them.

The purpose of building fallback options is to provide us not with another line of defence, or with a long-term response, but with an immediate response that can more or less do the job if there is network failure.

▲

The first thing to say about the fallback-option strategy is that it is emphatically *not* attempting to prevent networks from being damaged by attacks. The effort to construct defences is useful – indeed, necessary – to diminish the chances of successful attack. But fallback-option theory is based on recognizing that any presumption of perfect or perfectible defence is purely illusory, since human ingenuity and the forces of nature are both intrinsically unpredictable and there is bound to be a real, continuing, non-negligible chance that something, sometime – natural or artificial – will penetrate whatever defences are built, regardless of how much money, time, effort and intellect we apply to building defensive capabilities.

The second point about the fallback-option strategy follows directly from the first. Because the strategy presumes that perfect defence is impossible and assumes that a successful attack may occur, it does *not* depend upon predicting the type of attack that may succeed, or on estimating the probability of such successful attack. In one leap, it is freed from all the problems about interpreting statistics and identifying specific risks that inevitably afflict preventative defence planning in governments around the world. There is no need for the complicated and error-prone conversations between statisticians, administrators, politicians and the public about the likelihood of black-swan events that plague traditional defensive strategies, because no one engaged in formulating fallback options needs to ask how likely anything is to occur; the assumption is simply that a black-swan event *will* occur at some time, and the focus is on how to deal with it when it does occur. Likewise, the traditional preventative defence planning problem of finding someone who can 'think the unthinkable' and design defences against what are normally regarded as 'unthinkable' forms of attack evaporates because, in fallback-option planning, no one needs to worry about the nature of the attack; the whole aim is *not* to think that we can know, or even to speculate about what is likely to occur, but rather to assume that an *un*predicted form of black-swan attack will occur. The focus of a fallback-option plan is on how to maintain a semblance of normal operations immediately after such an attack has succeeded in knocking down the normal networks. The fallback strategy needs to work (to the extent of allowing us to 'get by') under all conceivable (even very unlikely) scenarios, and therefore needs to include a range of options suitable to different possible scenarios. The aim is to avoid prediction and worry exclusively about black-swan risks.

This point about the absence of prediction is crucial to an understanding of fallback-option thinking. To many administrators around the world, it is second nature to dwell on the question of what causes things to go wrong; they find it extraordinarily difficult to enter a mental world in which such questions become simply irrelevant. They can't easily refocus on working out how to deal with the consequences of things going wrong rather than how to prevent them going wrong. But what seems odd to the traditional administrators will seem perfectly natural to anyone who goes about their ordinary life in the way that most of us do. If the electricity in our home fails one evening, our most immediate question isn't 'why has this happened?' but 'what are we going to do about it?'; most of us keep either torches or mobile phones with in-built torches in our homes, so that we can at least see our way round if the lights do go off for a short period.

To take another example, if caring for our children becomes impossible one day because of an unforeseen set of circumstances, most parents have a fallback option ready to deploy – whether grandparents or siblings or friends or neighbours; we quite naturally build up informal, temporary systems that will keep the show on the road when normal life is disrupted in some significant way. For this purpose, it doesn't matter who or what has caused the problem, or how likely it was that it would happen. What matters is having some fallback on which we can all rely if and when the problem actually occurs – with the aim of ensuring that the problem does not turn into a disaster. Ordinary, sensible families do not hire teams of statisticians or technocrats to assess the likelihood and character of the events that might cause a power cut or that might make it impossible for us to get the children to school; they just take ordinary, sensible steps to ensure that it will be possible to carry on with something approaching normal life if they are deprived for a while of normal technologies, supports and services. At family-scale, this is the fallback-option strategy in action. The point of fallback-option planning in government and business is to get administrators and business leaders to stop thinking in abstract, administrative ways and to think for their nations in the way they think for their own homes and families.

The third, and heavily related, point about the fallback-option approach is that it is *not* attempting to enable life to continue with all its present advantages and conveniences after an attack has penetrated the network defences.

It is worth labouring this point, too, because in governmental and business circles around the world it seems very counter-intuitive to be aiming consciously at second-best solutions. Governments of all stripes like to provide their citizens with a guarantee that first-best solutions will always be made available, or at least with the illusion of such a guarantee. Well-meaning politicians (whether in multi-party liberal democracies or in highly organized single-party states such as China) like to be able to say to their people that if there is a superb technology in existence to deal with some problem, then that is the technology to which they will be given access. Just imagine the health service trying to explain to people that, instead of getting a brilliant life-enhancing drug, the patients will be coached in how to bear the pain; or the communications ministry telling people that they should put up with 2 mbps of broadband service when there is 100 mbps available from superior technology. The unpopularity generated by conscious admission of second-best offerings is so great that politicians and administrators learn not to make such admissions; indeed, they typically go to great lengths to present a rhetoric in which second-best simply doesn't figure. Businesses are the same: their leaders spend lifetimes avoiding any suggestion that they are offering their customers 'second best'.

But, when it comes to massive attack on fundamental networks, the fallback option is bound to be second best – because the first-best solution is the maintenance of the networks themselves, and the presumption of fallback-option planning is that these first-best networks will go down in some unpredicted way for some unpredicted reason. If the networks do go down, the fallback can't be to another first-best network, not only because it would be ruinously expensive to replicate the existing networks but also because it would be futile: whatever attack on the first-best networks has succeeded in putting them out of action is just as likely (or almost as likely) to put any replica out of action. Replication isn't really a fallback-option strategy at all; it is a form of defensive strategy based on the hope that whatever the attack is won't be powerful enough to knock down two nearly identical networks at the same time. But this depends on going back to all the questions that preoccupy traditional resilience planning: questions about the likely nature of the attacks and the likelihood of them succeeding. To provide a true fallback option that is maximally likely to be immune from whatever attack has succeeded in knocking down the first-best networks, we need something that is based on technology and human systems fundamentally different from those networks; and the different technology and systems will inevitably be inferior – because they will lack the characteristics that make the existing networks both so powerful and so vulnerable.

This point about second-best solutions is fundamental to fallback-option strategy. When constructing 'make-do-and-mend' systems that will just about get us by when the all-singing, all-dancing first-best technology fails, it is essential that the substitute systems are as different as possible from the first-best networks (so that they are maximally unlikely to be put out of operation by what-ever has knocked out the first-best networks). They must also be genuinely, totally independent from the first-best networks (so that they are both maximally unlikely to be polluted by any failure of those networks and are reliably able to function without recourse to those networks). Of course, such a 'make-do-and-mend' replacement system can't totally protect itself from all attack. It, too, like any system, will be open to attack. But the only hope is to design the fallback replacement system in a way that is as different as possible from the first-best existing networks, so that the fallback system is maximally invulnerable to whatever has attacked the existing networks. This means using technology as divergent as possible from the tech-nology contained in the existing networks – which in turn means relinquishing any attempt to replicate the huge efficiency gains that arise from convergent and intercon-nected networks. Only by making that conscious sacrifice can we hope to permit the fallback to operate wholly independently from the existing networks.

So our aim in structuring the fallback option needs be exactly the opposite of the aim of those who design the first-best networks on which we normally rely. In fallback-option planning, instead of seeking to optimize efficiency by maximizing convergence and interconnectedness, we need on the contrary to optimize the chances of surviving whatever attack has affected the first-best networks by maximizing the number of independent sources of survival. We need, in other words, to maximize *div*ergence rather than *con*vergence. This will have two effects, one good and one bad. The good effect is that the minimally interconnected fallback system can be designed to minimize the likelihood of being knocked out by whatever attack has knocked out the existing networks. The bad effect is that the minimally interconnected fallback system will be very much second-best: it will by design lack all of the huge advantages that come from highly integrated and convergent networks. *In other words, in fallback-option planning, the aim is to design in inefficiency.* This will seem counter-intuitive to most administrators and politicians (and indeed journalists and business people) in most countries. But there is nothing counter-intuitive about it if one enters the mental world of fallback options.

If a farmer is crucially dependent on getting messages

back to his farmhouse from distant fields, and if he knows that the mobile signal in his rural area has an unpredictable propensity to fail, then using an old-fashioned, analogue walkie-talkie may be a highly rational fallback option. Old-fashioned walkie-talkies are unlikely to be endangered by the types of event that might cause his mobile signal to disappear for a period, because they don't rely on any of the equipment that forms the mobile telephone system. But point-to-point analogue walkie-talkies are never going to compete with modern digital communications on the basis of their general effectiveness or efficiency; they won't get anywhere near. So, by taking the walkie-talkie with him, the farmer is consciously accepting an additional cost and is consciously adopting a fallback option that designs in inefficiency by comparison with his normal, up-to-date communications system. But his strategy may make perfect sense – since it provides a replacement fallback that comes as near as possible to being completely different from, and to being completely disconnected from, modern communications.

It is not an accident or a slip of the pen when I refer to society's first-best networks (such as the mobile networks) going out of operation for 'a period', because the next point about fallback options is that they are meant specifically to cover only a short period. We are talking, here, about a replacement that is consciously temporary rather than permanent. The aim of the fallback-option approach is emphatically *not* to provide a lasting alternative to the existing, convergent technologies. Rather, the aim of the second-best fallback system is to provide something that just about does the basic job during the relatively brief time that it typically takes for the first-best networks to be restored following a successful attack. Of course, if the attack is big enough, there may not be a capacity for such early restoration: if we are subjected to nuclear Armageddon, or the sun tomorrow defies all predictions by expanding and swallowing up the Earth (as it will eventually do, but is not likely to do tomorrow), then fallback-option strategies won't save us. But nor will anything else, other than leaving this planet and going to another one.

Fallback-option strategies are designed to deal not with mass Earth-evacuation following events that are in themselves cataclysmic, but rather with the relatively restricted events that wouldn't be cataclysmic (and, by the way, wouldn't be capable of occurring) if we didn't have the highly interconnected, convergent networks on which we have come to depend so heavily.

We are talking here about the problems of success. We need to recognize that the vulnerabilities to which we are increasingly exposed arise only because of the increasingly universal deployment of intelligent, interconnected, convergent networks which represent, for most other purposes, a massive leap forward. It is the risk of disaster arising from *any* failure of these networks (due to our continuous expectation of, and increasing dependence upon, their functioning) that we are trying to prevent through fallback-option strategies. In these non-Armageddon circumstances, the problem isn't, typically, that no recovery is possible; it's that (as the story in this book illustrates) even a short period of non-operation during recovery could turn a problem into a disaster. So what we need is a 'make-do-and-mend' solution that more or less holds things together for long enough to enable the fundamental networks to be brought back into operation.

This sort of thinking doesn't go on only at family-scale (the householder with a torch to see in a power cut, the parents with fallback childcare arrangements, the farmer with the walkie-talkie). It also happens at local community level. In my own village in Dorset, a highly rural part of the southwest of England, we have a network of minor roads and tiny lanes, many of which are too narrow for two cars to pass one another except at passing places, and many of which also climb steep hills. When we have a snowy winter (perhaps one winter in ten at present), these small roads and lanes become impassable for anyone without a tractor or four-wheel drive. Major roads are cleared of snow by the county council, but there are so many of these little roads that it is impossible for the county council to clear them in reasonable time at reasonable cost. And some of these roads are inessential, as long as others can be made usable – because most villages have several ways in and out. So, instead of trying to predict whether it will snow, or (even more absurdly) trying to prevent it snowing, or (too expensively) setting up a new county-wide snow-clearance programme for the narrow roads, there are just some bins with salt in them that the locals can use to make at least one road into the village passable, if cars go slowly. This is a classic case of a second-best fallback option: cheap, simple, far-from-perfect, and based on the assumption that the normal network will be disrupted for a period by events which we have not managed to prevent – but serviceable enough to let something like normal life carry on, albeit with a great deal less convenience. One could find multitudes of similar examples all over the world, typically in communities which, for one reason or another, have not lost the habit of self-reliance. Often, these communities are either less industrially developed or more rural and more isolated than the cities and suburbs of the rich world. Although they, too, normally depend to a degree on regional, national and global networks, they are sufficiently sceptical about the priority they are likely to be accorded in a moderate national or international crisis to feel the need for second-best, self-help, fallback systems. And they organize these systems without thinking that they are doing anything unusual or remarkable. They would be amazed to find themselves described as being at the forefront of fallback-option strategy; they are just doing what comes naturally.

The challenge, at national and global scale is not, therefore, to invent an unprecedented new way of dealing with failure of the networks on which we rely. Rather, the challenge is to find a way of persuading national and global administrators and politicians, as well as those who influence citizens and service-users across the world, to mimic the natural inclinations of families and small, isolated communities.

We need the administrators, politicians, business leaders and community leaders to remove themselves for a time from their statisticians, complex models and traditional preventative defence planning and start thinking of themselves not as overworked officials in high-pressure offices but as members of families and communities, as people who, like the rest of us, are increasingly vulnerable to network failure.

Businesses need to play their part because they, too, are vulnerable to network failure – at least, all those businesses that do not have the 'natural fallback options' of closing down temporarily or of continuing operation on a scaled-back basis during the period of network failure. We need to ask: what should be done by businesses (in sectors such as food and pharmaceuticals) whose own vulnerability to network failure will quickly be translated into disaster for the vulnerable individuals who depend critically upon their services?

Let us deal first with those businesses whose exposure is purely commercial, and whose disruption will *not* translate into wider social damage.

Clearly, there is a choice to be made by the businesses themselves. It is their commercial futures, rather than society's ability to function, that are at risk; so it is for them rather than the state to decide how far to invest in precautionary measures. Equally clearly, these businesses have a balancing act to perform – since there will be costs involved in protecting their ability to carry on selling their goods or services during a period of network failure, and these costs will need to be balanced against the loss of revenue that would arise for them if they were unable to function during such a period. Nor is there any one-size-fits-all answer to this question. Those businesses for which the maintenance of thin margins is critical from day to day will inevitably have a different view than those for which margins and returns are rich; likewise, those which can implement extremely cheap fallback 'analogue' solutions to a temporary but persistent collapse of digital networks will make very different decisions from those businesses for which fallback arrangements are hideously expensive and complicated.

There is only one truth that can be universally applied

to such businesses: they all have good reason to engage consciously in this balancing exercise, because their long-term futures may depend upon it. And, of course, if they all do this thinking, and if each makes decisions based upon the outcome of that thinking, our economy as a whole will be more resilient than it would be if they *either* over-invest in precautionary action that is excessively costly *or* heedlessly avoid establishing cheap and effective fallback solutions that would allow them to maintain operations and revenue generation during a period of network failure.

In other words, this is a classic case of the wisdom of the market: many sub-critical businesses, each making what appear to them rational and balanced decisions after consciously considering the risks and costs, are more likely to arrive at an aggregate result that is rational than any amount of centralized planning.

But, even here, there is a role for the state – because it is in the interest of the economy and society as a whole that we should be as resilient as we can be without disproportionate present cost. There is, in other words, what economists call an 'externality' here: businesses that act in their own long-term interest by becoming more resilient through adopting sensible fallback options thereby also benefit the rest of us. Given that the achievement of this resilience depends on the judgements made by a multitude of individual sub-critical businesses, it is in the public interest that the business community should be properly informed. In other words, the people running businesses need to know about the costs and benefits of fallback options that will enable them to keep going in the face of network failure. It would therefore be entirely appropriate for the state to help this process of rational consideration by providing straightforward information of a relevant kind to businesses that would otherwise find it difficult to obtain such information or would not seek it.

Surprisingly, I am not aware of any state in the world that currently does provide such information to business. Even those states that are most concerned and knowledgeable about network failure (such as the UK, the USA, China, Russia, South Korea and some of the Baltic states) show no sign of concerning themselves with the fate of sub-critical businesses in such an event, even to the extent of providing a 'nudge' to the market.

It would be relatively easy to cure this particular disease. In the case of the so-called 'millennium bug' (which never materialized to anything like the expected extent), huge and ironically successful attempts were made by governments across the world to alert businesses to the issue; similarly, many governments are now quite rightly and energetically alerting businesses of all kinds to the threat of cyber-attack, with a view to ensuring that those businesses consider how much effort and money it is rational for them to spend on protection against such attacks – the work of the UK's National Cyber Security Centre is a leading example. It would not take much for governments to take similar steps to ensure that sub-critical businesses across the economy are alerted to the possible effects of network failure and have the information they need to enable them to make a balanced judgement of whether it is commercially rational for them to construct 'analogue' fallback solutions. But the bigger and far more pressing problem is that governments are not yet acting to create fallback solutions even for those non-network businesses that, far from being 'sub-critical', are in fact providing crucial hidden public services. In part, no doubt, this is because most governments define 'critical national infra-structure' much too narrowly – restricting the scope to government itself, public authorities, traditional 'public services' (like the health service) and the public utilities such as energy and telecoms. The result is that busi-nesses participating in the food-supply industries and the pharmaceutical industries, on which many lives depend, get left off the list. For many purposes, this is perfectly sensible: an interruption of a day or so in food supply or pharmaceuticals will certainly not cause any appalling consequences if the public authorities, the traditional 'public services' and the regulated networks are still oper-ating to pick up the pieces. So it makes sense to attend most closely to the provision of fallback options for the traditional and narrowly defined elements of 'critical national infrastructure'.

However, under circumstances such as those described in our parable – where the nation faces several days of systemic network failure, our resilience as a society is hugely diminished if the hidden public services such as the chains that supply food or pharmaceuticals are out of commission. Indeed, the very fact that the networks at the core of our economy and society are not functioning normally under such circumstances makes the continuity of the other businesses that constitute the hidden public services even *more* important than normal. It is exactly under such circumstances of network failure that the most vulnerable people, who might otherwise be able to reach or be reached by the public authorities or the traditional public services, are least likely to be able to receive help from these quarters and are therefore most likely to be dependent on the hidden public services. This is true even if fallback options are in place to enable the public authorities, the traditional 'public services' and the regulated networks to provide a scaled-down service. It becomes even more true if service from these quarters fails entirely in a particular area of the country.

This brings out an important general point about the way in which fallback-option planning can and should be used to provide *layers of fallback solutions* rather than just one set of fallback solutions for individual parts of the converging network of networks on which we increasingly rely.

A good way to think of modern economies and societies is to picture them as a series of spheres of ascending diameters, with the smallest sphere nestling within the next, that one nestling within a larger sphere and so forth – a bit like a set of Russian dolls. But, in this case, each of the spheres, instead of being solid like the surface of one of the Russian dolls, is composed of an intricate web of criss-crossing strings. Each intersection-point of the strings that constitute the smallest sphere at the inner core of the multi-layered ball is connected with a corresponding point or points on the sphere that surrounds it. And this pattern of complex connections between the spheres continues right up to the outer surface of the ball – so that the whole thing presents the appearance of a near-solid mass of criss-crossing strings going in all directions.

The strings represent relationships or networks. The nodes or intersections between them represent institutions or individuals. Just as we live on the outer surface of the Earth, so we live our lives on the outer surface of the ball of relationships and networks, each of us living at the intersection of a multitude of surface strings that represent our connections, direct and indirect, with a multitude of other persons through a welter of relationships. But the whole of this surface-life depends on the multitude of connections that the outer sphere, on which we live, has with the institutions (for example, the businesses) on the sphere beneath. These institutions depend, in turn, upon the connections that they have with the even more fundamental and densely interconnected institutions (for example, the public services and the public authorities) on the third sphere down. And so, at last, we come to the smallest and most tightly bound of the spherical webs, which constitutes the inner core of the ball – the network of converging networks, on which directly or indirectly all of the relationships within the outer spheres (and hence all of the relationships that constitute our lives on the outermost surface of the ball) depend.

This image of modern life brings out the extent to which the resilience of our society and economy now relies not just on the strength of the inner core (the network of networks), or even just on the ability of the institutions such as public services to rely on analogue fallback options which will continue to work when their links with the core networks fail, but also on the ability of the businesses operating at the third level up to rely on their own separate fallback options when connections with the core networks and public services fail.

So, for true social and economic resilience, we need layers of fallback options – at the level of individual lives, at the level of 'ordinary businesses', at the level of businesses that deliver hidden public services, at the level of public authorities and traditional public services, and (of course) at the level of the fundamental networks themselves. The paradox is that, as everything increasingly depends on a core network of converging networks, and hence becomes more intricately interconnected with everything else, each part of our society and economy increasingly needs the capacity *in extremis* to operate independently of all the things with which it is normally interconnected. Just as digital networks require analogue fallback options, everyday convergence is resilient only if it can be replaced by a fallback to divergence when things go wrong.

This requirement – that complex and highly convergent digital societies should be able to fall back *in extremis* to simpler, more divergent analogue ways of living – is a message that elected politicians in liberal democracies need to take seriously, because the citizens who elect them will expect them to do so. As the parable in this book indicates, it is not only anarchy or invasion that threatens the safety of the citizen. Disease, natural disasters, economic crises and failures of technology also constitute serious threats. And network failures can make all of these kinds of threats either more likely, or more severe in their impacts. Citizens therefore understandably expect their governments and legislatures not only to protect them against each of these but also to protect them from the consequences of network failure, at least to a reasonable extent. In fact, the history of disasters in modern societies suggests that citizens expect even more from their governments when dealing with natural or artificial catastrophes that occur in peacetime than when dealing with war or anarchy.

In conditions of war or widespread violence, societies tend to be united by a common enemy. By contrast, in peacetime crises, there is often no obvious enemy – and the enemy can therefore all too easily become the government or even, under extreme circumstances, the state itself – if the government or state is seen to have let the people down by failing to protect them from the risk that has become a dreadful reality.

There are interesting and important examples of this contrast in attitudes afforded by recent global history. In the UK, there is the contrast between the Second World War and the Depression of the early 1930s. In India, there is the contrast between partition and Bhopal.

By any standards, the pain and suffering inflicted on the world by the 1939–45 war, with millions of deaths and huge numbers of casualties, was vastly greater than the economic disaster caused by the Depression of the early 1930s. Even Britain, which suffered far fewer casualties than Jews in Germany or Russians in Russia, fared much worse in the Second World War than it did in the Depression, which damaged the lives of multitudes but (if we do not count suicide) directly killed no one.

In the same way, the humanitarian catastrophe of partition between India and Pakistan (and in particular between the two halves of the Punjab) in 1947, which killed somewhere between 200,000 and 2 million people, was wholly out of proportion to the industrial disaster that occurred when toxic methyl isocyanate gas leaked from the Union Carbide chemical plant in Bhopal in 1984, killing between 4,000 and 16,000 people.

But the political fallout from the Second World War in Britain or partition in India was far less exaggerated than the political consequences that flowed from the 1930s Depression or the Bhopal industrial disaster. Although the British voted for Attlee rather than Churchill after the Second World War, this represented an ideological shift rather than retribution: no one spoke about it as a rebuke for Churchill's war leadership, and – as his subsequent re-election indicated – his reputation remained untarnished by the death toll; the blame for the casualties of war fell on the common enemy: Hitler. Likewise, there is little if any sign in the historical literature of either Indians or Pakistanis blaming their own Congress Party or Muslim League leaderships for the appalling inter-communal violence of partition in India: once again, the blame fell on common enemies: either the British colonial power, or the opposing Muslim or Hindu communities.

In stark contrast, the political effect of the Depression following the 1929 crash in the UK, where no obvious common enemy could be identified, was dramatic: the Labour Party (which had been elected to form a minority government with Liberal support just before the crash) went down to a resounding defeat in the ensuing 1931 general election. The government became the enemy.

Likewise, although the initial shock of the Bhopal disaster just three weeks before the 1984 general election in India does not appear to have had any marked political effect, the sustained criticism of the Congress government over its handling of Bhopal in the years that followed was undoubtedly a significant factor contributing to the decisive defeat of the Congress government in the 1989 national election – and in Madhya Pradesh itself (the state in which Bhopal lies), the effect was far more marked; Congress, which had held forty out of forty seats in the state legislature, was reduced to eight seats, with a massive swing to the Bharatiya Janata Party, which had campaigned aggressively on the issue. Once again, a significant share of the blame for the civil catastrophe fell on the government.

One of the conclusions to draw from this is, of course, the Machiavellian point that governments should, for their own safety, take considerable pains to ensure that the safety of the populations over which they govern are not put at risk by events where no obvious external enemy can be identified as the prime cause. But one can also draw a deeper conclusion about democratic sentiment and about the legitimate expectations of a population. Electorates will tolerate extraordinary privations and extraordinary death tolls if they are united in the face of foreign foes or enemies in civil warfare, without blaming their leaders, so long as the ostensible purpose of the conflict is fulfilled – because they can believe that their leaders are 'on their side' in such conflict. But the same electorates will find it difficult to tolerate even substantially less severe catastrophes if they come to believe that their leaders have left them exposed to risks that could and should have been prevented from affecting their lives. People feel that they have a legitimate expectation that government will anticipate and manage such risks.

Serious, persistent network failure falls clearly into this latter category. It may or may not be possible in a given case to identify an enemy who is responsible for the network failure. In the story told in this book, the cause is natural rather than human, so there is no enemy to find. In other cases of network failure, such as those caused by cyber-attack, it may prove difficult or even impossible to identify the enemy. In cases where there is a clear and identifiable human cause of the network failure, the public may identify with the government insofar as it and its agencies are trying to deal with the responsible enemy; but there is no reason to suppose that the public would easily forgive the government if there was no human cause, or if the enemy cannot be identified.

If the result of a lack of fallback options is only the loss of public confidence in a particular group of ministers, this (as opposed to the consequences of the catastrophe itself) is not a fundamental issue for the nation. But when legitimate expectations of civil security are not met on a major scale, as in the story told in this book, one cannot guarantee that popular sentiment will sweep away only the particular group of politicians who happen to be in charge at the time of the disaster. When one compares the death toll imagined in our story with the actual death tolls caused by the Great Depression in the UK or by the Bhopal disaster in India, one is brought face to face with the fact that serious, persistent network failure in the absence of any effective fallback options could plausibly cause a civil disaster with consequences unseen since the invention of modern medicine and modern public health systems. There can be no guarantee that such an event would merely destabilize the government as pictured in the story; it could plausibly threaten to destabilize the state itself. Liberal democracies are fragile, demagoguery is latent, and there is every reason not to test whether the liberal democratic system would prove robust in the face of calamity on this scale. Well-organized one-party states of the kind we see, for example, in China are if anything even more fragile; again, one would not want to test whether either their organization or their stability would be sustainable in such an event.

So, notwithstanding the horror of hundreds of thousands of frail, elderly people dying, there is something even deeper and longer lasting at stake here than the immediate effects imagined in our story: namely, the perceived long-run legitimacy of the state. But there is another, equally fundamental, issue – the legitimacy of modern technology and the global structures within which it has emerged.

Network technology and the global structures that sustain it are such huge engines of progress that they can all too easily seem permanent and unchallengeable. But anyone inclined to regard them in this way is making the same sort of mistake that led many well-intentioned liberals to under-estimate Donald Trump. Technological progress and global free-market structures have many friends but also many enemies, and the risks as well as the rewards are now global. For as long as these technologies and structures contribute to the quality of life of almost the whole population, they are likely to continue to attract sufficient goodwill to overcome the suspicions of many citizens. But the goodwill of the majority is highly conditional. Unmanaged network disaster could at any time tilt one country or even the whole world into revisionism and reversion. We should not forget the religiously endorsed horror of new technology which characterized much of the Middle Ages in Europe, and which held back human development for centuries. Also, under such a calamity, there would be no shortage of illib-eral politicians willing to play on the xenophobia that is always latent by pointing to the connection between the consequences of network failure and what they would describe as over-dependence on the global Internet, global banking and global communications. They would quickly draw attention to the obvious implication that such open-textured global networks should be abandoned in favour of nationally based fortresses.

As well as being hugely important in itself, this risk of technological reversion arising from any episode of unmanaged serious and persistent network failure is a metaphor for another even wider problem. There are many areas of technology today which offer the prospect of transformative advance, but which can also conjure up visions of Frankenstein if the risks associated with them are not properly managed. The emergence of artificial intelligence, of microscopic organic factories based on stunning advances in molecular biology, and of genetic modification or bio-engineering of human beings are just three current examples of this genre.

Governments the world over have recognized that resistance to such technological leaps is constricting, impoverishing and ultimately futile. They have also recognized that sensible regulation of these frontiers of science is crucial. But the discussion around the world, and particularly in those countries which contain the lion's share of the emerging technologies, has not moved beyond a worryingly old-fashioned debate about the shape and nature of the regulation. Just as the conversation about global networks has hitherto focused almost exclusively on the need to build defences against predicted attacks rather than on the need for fallback options in the event of unpredicted network failure, so the conversation about regulation of the emerging technologies has failed to recognize that regulatory structures, while certainly necessary, are not sufficient. In the transformative technologies now emerging, as in the network technologies that have already become established, we need more than protective defences and defensive regulation. If we are to engender and sustain genuine trust, we need to establish how to move back a step if and when, for whatever (possibly wholly unforeseen) reason, such temporary retreat should become necessary. It is one thing to advance into the unknown, confident that one can easily find the way back temporarily to a well-understood terrain, quite another to commit to the journey with no established route back to safety.

6

A DIFFICULT CHOICE

By the time Bill Donoghue arrived back at Yeovil Hospital, having settled his mother-in-law in her favourite chair with her current novel and wrapped in as many layers of clothing as he could persuade her to wear, it was 11 a.m.

The scene that greeted him as he re-entered Yeovil and reached the hospital car park was much less orderly than it had been in the early hours. As well as the ambulances, still queued up by the entrance to the A&E unit, private cars were now spilling out of the car park itself and were strewn around all conceivable spaces. No doubt, their drivers had taken comfort from the fact that, even if any parking restrictions applied on New Year's Day, there would be no parking wardens to enforce them.

Inside the hospital, it was warm but the crowd, which had seemed large the night before, had now grown to a scale that he had seen only in airports where thousands of passengers had been stranded by foul weather. People everywhere were jostling for space, attempting to move through those already encamped. With considerable difficulty, he made his way into the A&E area and attempted to find someone who could take a message to Elaine. It was about twenty minutes before she emerged – looking every bit as exhausted as he had expected.

'I've got to go back in a minute. It's mayhem in there. We are all staying in post until mid-afternoon so we can double up with the morning shift. It's the only way we can see of dealing with the numbers before the whole system collapses under its own weight. How is mum?'

'She's fine. But the house is cold, and we can't cook anything or call anyone or get any news. I am frankly amazed that she is taking it all so stoically. She seems to have a touching faith that you and I will make sure it all turns out OK.'

'There are times when it pays to be an absurd optimist – and I suppose this is one of them. I remember when I was a child and I fell down a well in the neighbour's garden. My dad went practically mad with angst; I could hear him rushing around the garden calling cluelessly for help. But mum just peered down at me, enquired gently whether I seemed to have broken anything (which I hadn't) and then assured me authoritatively that some wholly indefinite 'they' would undoubtedly get me out "once your father has calmed down enough to make a call". After the fire brigade had been called in to winch me out, she showed no sign whatsoever of continuing concern. All in a day's play! I suppose that's the attitude that has carried her through today. I just wish some of my patients in there had the same stoical attitude. Unfortunately, they are mainly in my father's mould.'

'She certainly has the right spirit. One of the reasons I made the very sensible decision to marry you is that you have inherited it. And I'm sure that you are doing a magnificent job with the patients in there, however difficult and worried they are. But the fact is that your mother's optimism won't actually save her from starvation or hypothermia, and we've still got to deal with the practical problem of a frail, old woman living alone in a house with nothing functioning normally – in fact, not much functioning at all.'

A look of agony passed across Elaine's exhausted face.

'Oh, Bill. I don't have any constructive suggestions. I'm completely locked in here. The rest of the team couldn't possibly cope if I left now. Almost all of them have children or elderly relatives that they're worried about; but, as I say, they are all staying in post. This is the NHS at its magnificent best. I'm afraid there's no way I'm going to be able to leave the hospital until this is all over. Somehow, you'll just have to manage her. Can you take her with you to London?'

'Only if she will come. You know what she thinks of

London – and of long car journeys. I can try explaining everything you've just said about why you can't come home, and I expect she will happily accept that; she believes in everyone doing their duty. But she is very inclined to regard all my fussing around her as needless and neurotic. I'm sure her personal default option will be to remain put in Somerset, sitting in a room that just gets colder and colder, with less and less to eat.'

Elaine smiled weakly: 'You have spent your whole life persuading difficult people to do difficult things. And this is a moment when that particular skill is exactly what is needed. I'm afraid I'm going to have to love you and leave you. And I hope to see you and my mum hale and hearty in some part of England at some future time when we've all got through this, and I've caught up on about a century of lost sleep.'

As usual, Elaine's irony was just a way of making her fundamental good sense less didactic. She was, of course, quite right. She was, literally, dealing with issues of life and death, even more pressing than his duty to help restore orderly financial markets.

The Donoghues would just have to do their best and try to make the least worst choices under the circumstances.

As Bill set off for East Coker, he turned on the car radio in an absent-minded attempt to calm his nerves with some soothing music. There was nothing but static on the multitude of digital channels. Silly of him to have forgotten momentarily that the electricity supply for the broadcasters was down – all the more so as he now dimly recalled being told about this in some resilience briefing at the Bank. Apparently, a decision had been made not to provide back-up generators for the main UK transmitters because the costs of providing such back-up would be prohibitive. He remembered being slightly worried at the time about what would happen in an emergency, but it hadn't preoccupied him for more than a fleeting moment. And now, everyone would be discovering exactly what the effects of that short-sighted decision really were. In the old days, of course, with short-wave or even medium-wave AM radios, it would have been possible at least to pick up foreign broadcasts from stations unaffected by whatever had happened to the UK electricity grid. But, with the complete switchover to digital broadcasting, those days were long past.

In the absence of any calming tunes, he began to think about what the virtual disappearance of short-wave radio would mean for communications between the UK and the rest of the world. Out there, somewhere, there must be some remaining old-fashioned radio hams with short-wave transmitters and receivers. But did they rely on mains electricity? And, even if they were battery-run, how would anyone at the centre of government track them down, especially under current circumstances? So, unless there were fibres separately lit with comms systems separately backed up in case of grid failure, there really wouldn't be any communications outwards or inwards from or to the UK. Of course, satellites could have substituted for fibre under normal conditions. But it was abundantly clear that whatever had knocked out the grid had also knocked out the satellites; otherwise, his GPS would be working. This conclusion kept circulating round his mind as he left the outskirts of Yeovil behind him and headed out into the countryside. It seemed almost unimaginable that there could be this degree of failure in forward-planning. But he couldn't see any reason to doubt that the UK really was cut off.

As he turned onto the West Coker Road at the roundabout junction with the A37, he was distracted from this rather disturbing line of thought by a commotion to his right. A group of young men seemed to be smashing in the window of the little shop on the corner of the road leading back up to the Lynx Trading Estate. Was this, he wondered, a foretaste of things to come? Were some people who couldn't buy whatever they needed just going to help themselves to it instead? He remembered hearing that this sort of thing had happened after hurricanes in the USA. But was it going to start happening on a major scale in Somerset? Or were these just exuberant youths who had reacted to the unusual circumstances by drinking too much of whatever alcohol they had to hand,

and who were now on an inebriated rampage in the pretty certain knowledge that the police would be preoccupied elsewhere?

To judge by the amount of noise they were making, the drunken-party hypothesis seemed likely to be valid – and that didn't really tell one much about how the rest of the population would respond. But he could just about imagine that, if the black-out went on much longer, some people would have serious food shortages. Of course, shopkeepers could open up and provide bare essentials at least during daylight hours, and at least until they ran out of stock. But would they be sufficiently generous to give food away? Or sufficiently trusting to accept hand-written IOUs in place of the electronic transfers that all transactions normally required? In particular, would such informal credit be given to those vulnerable and relatively impoverished people who needed it most? And if these same people didn't have friends or neighbours able to help them out, what were they to do other than beg or steal?

He found these thoughts so troubling that his pre-occupation with keeping Elaine's mother safe and sound ceased, for a while, to dominate his consciousness. But, as he drove on through West Coker, he began to re-focus on the task ahead. How was he going to persuade his mother-in-law to abandon her cherished country cottage and make the unwelcome trip to the unloved capital? Was it better to appeal to her sense of self-preservation? Or should he try to persuade her that his promise to Elaine simply had to be kept? Or was it best to big up his own anxiety, in an effort to convince her that her staying put would reduce him to a gibbering wreck and hence prevent him from doing his important work in London anything like as well as he needed to, for the whole country's sake? It wasn't by any means easy to tell which line of attack was most likely to work. Perhaps he should try all three approaches, one after the other.

It was with these thoughts swirling around in his head that he turned off the A30 towards East Coker.

7

MYTHS AND REALITIES

It isn't only those like Bill Donoghue who may find themselves in the future dealing with difficult choices in the event of a network meltdown. If we're to minimize the chance of such future crises, our governments and business leaders need to make some difficult choices right now.

Meeting this challenge requires emotional intelligence more than high-flown technical skill: the people with the required technical skills are available if one knows what questions to ask them and if one can get those who hold power to ask those questions. The trick is to get the right mental attitudes instilled so that they do ask such questions.

Modern public choice theory developed by the Nobel-Prize-winning economist James Buchanan teaches us that office-holders – so far from acting purely as faceless bureaucrats in the utterly dispassionate and supremely efficient way fondly imagined by nineteenth-century sociologists like Max Weber – actually turn out to be human beings like the rest of us. This should not be a surprise. When people come into the office in the morning, they don't leave behind them the motivations that they had when they went to bed at home the evening before. Certainly, they want, by and large, to do their office-jobs conscientiously. But they also want to do them in ways that will advance their own standing and earn the respect of colleagues, families, friends as well as the society in which they live. So we cannot hope to get them to think afresh about network fragility just by administering lectures. Instead, we have to find ways of persuading them that they can think such fresh thoughts without being dismissed as impractical cranks.

No doubt, the precise methods that are most likely to make this happen will differ in different jurisdictions at different times – depending on the prevailing political and administrative cultures. But there are some common obstacles that will need to be overcome in any basically benign administration anywhere in the world.

Wasted money

The accusation that constructing fallback options is a 'waste of money' may be based on any one of numerous kinds of scepticism. These range from the bold and broad belief that the first-best networks are never going to fail in the first place, down to highly specific and practical concerns about the practicality of particular fallback solutions.

The point of the story in this book is that, if we go on allowing ourselves to be beguiled by the 'it won't happen anyway' brigade or worn down by the 'it's all too difficult' doom-mongers, sooner or later we may come bitterly to regret our inaction. When the networks do fail, we won't have even a semi-operational 'make-do-and-mend' alternative ready for use. But, of course, stories are just stories. Anyone can make them up. So the sceptics come back to the question: 'why would we want to waste real money on enabling ourselves to deal with something that may or may not happen, when we could be spending the money either on defences that will make it less likely to happen or on some other real and present item that will improve the lives of real people right now?'

The problem is not that we can't answer this question. The problem is, rather, that the sceptical administrator or politician may not be persuaded by theoretically robust answers to a legitimate intellectual doubt – because the essential feeling that lies behind the 'wasted money' thesis (and it is a feeling, not a thought) is that spending money on fallback options is something that will be impossible to explain convincingly to the general public because it is too speculative. In other words, administrators and politicians regard this, at least partly, as a *communications* problem.

The right response to a communications challenge isn't more theoretical argument: it is to develop a proper communications strategy. So the emotionally intelligent way of persuading the sceptical administrators and politicians who worry about the 'wasted money' argument is not to try to defeat the argument intellectually, but to explain to them how the need for fallback options can be communicated to the media and the public.

In part, of course, this requires a long-term effort of explanation – which is where the story and the analysis in this book come in. Over time, books like this one can help to spread the message that there is a problem, and that cheap and cheerful fallback options can provide a half-way reasonable solution. And if that message gradually percolates through formal media and social media, engendering discussions, seminars, blogs and the rest of it, part of the communications challenge will be overcome naturally, since (as with anything that gets widely discussed for long enough) more and more of the public and more and more of those appearing in the media will find themselves assuming that it is sane – indeed sensible – to worry about all of this.

But my own experience suggests that we can actually make progress even faster than this long-term communications strategy would suggest – at least in countries like the UK. Literally as I wrote the last few pages, an email arrived on my smartphone, inviting me to a seminar on 'Crisis Leadership – the search for the perfect response to extreme events'. This might have seemed like a massive coincidence, were it not for the fact that these sorts of events are going on all the time in London. And every time I mention at some gathering of the great and good that I am concerned about how we deal with black-swan events causing network failure, at least one of those present assures me that he or she is even more worried than I am. So I discern that we have already got to the point where, at least in UK academic and security circles, serious and experienced people are recognizing that this is a sensible area for discussion. What's more, in the UK, we have already got to the point where some very senior ministers, parliamentarians and officials have recognized the need for fallback alternatives in the event of network failure – ensuring that this isn't regarded as lunacy within government either.

So the ground, at least in the UK, is fertile. But we need to cultivate it. And then we need to use the UK as an example to show the sceptics in other governments that the vital points can be communicated without the communicator being regarded as especially eccentric. Once that message has been absorbed, there will be much less tendency to argue that constructing fallback options is a waste of money, and those remaining sceptics who do continue to argue this will be much less likely to gain traction inside their governments.

The myth of cost–benefit analysis

So much for the emotional fear of spending money on fallback solutions whose rationale is supposedly incommunicable.

This leaves us with the remorselessly rational approach of people in the finance ministries and auditing functions of governments. They have been trained by economists to conduct so-called 'rational cost–benefit analysis', based on applying a 'discount rate' to future costs and benefits.

The simplest way of grasping the idea of a discount rate is to imagine that Mr A has promised to give you £101 a year from now, and Mr B has promised to give you £100 today. How should you calculate which is the better offer? Answer: you should allow for the fact that, if you put Mr B's £100 into a completely safe bank account for a year, it will give you £2 of interest and you will still have the £100 at the end of the year – so Mr B's offer of £100 today is better than Mr A's offer of £101 a year from now. Another way to describe this is that Mr A's offer of £101 a year from now should be 'discounted' by the interest rate in order to get a fair comparison with the present value of Mr B's £100 today. So you should divide Mr A's offer by 1.02, where the '0.02' represents the 2% interest rate – and, at that discount rate, Mr A's offer of £101 a year from now is worth only £101/1.02 = £99.02 today, which is obviously less than Mr B's £100 in ready money today.

But, of course, not all investments are as safe as bank accounts or government bonds, so the economists have refined the idea of discounting to allow not only for the time value of money (as in the case of Mr A and Mr B) but also for the degree of risk attaching to a benefit or cost in the future.

Imagine, for example, that you believe there is a 10% chance of Mr A not in fact coming up with his £101 a year from now. In that case, his offer is much less attractive than Mr B's £100 today, which you can see he has in his hand to give you right now. Economists represent this difference by adding to the 2% discount rate (representing the government bond interest) a further discount rate of 10% to allow for the risk of not getting Mr A's £101 a year from now. So they divide Mr A's £101 by 1.12 instead of 1.02 – making it worth only £101/1.12 = £90.18, a good deal less than Mr B's £100 in ready money today.

Finally, economists have pointed out that, where costs or benefits lie far in the future, the discount rate should be compounded. So, for example, if Mr A is actually offering you his £101 two years away, then you should divide it by 1.02^2 to allow for two years of interest that you can earn on Mr B's £100 if you take it today, or by 1.12^2 to allow also for the compound risk that Mr A won't pay.

Once equipped with this idea of discount rates that allow both for the time value of money and for the risk attaching to benefits and costs in the future, economists feel that they have a way of assessing the comparative 'net present value' of any set of expected costs and benefits over any future period given any set of risks and any given time value of money.

The economists' principle is simple. They assess the *costs* of any given proposed course of action, discounting costs incurred in later years by an appropriate discount rate compared with costs incurred in earlier years. Then they do the same for the *benefits* of the proposed course of action. They recommend taking the course of action in question only if (a) the discounted benefits exceed the discounted costs and (b) the extent of the net benefit is sufficiently great to rank the course of action ahead of other net-beneficial actions in other areas in which one could invest the money.

For many purposes, such cost–benefit analysis is genuinely rational. If you are trying to decide whether to buy a new carpet or keep the old one for longer and spend the money instead on a new hoover, it makes sense to do this kind of comparison, working out for yourself how much each item costs and what benefits each item will bring – with particular emphasis on immediate costs and benefits, but with a sensible eye also to the longer term. Likewise, if a department of transport is trying to decide what roads it should build or upgrade in a given year, it makes abundant sense to develop good estimates of the costs and benefits to the economy across the coming years (with appropriate discount rates to reflect the risks and the time value of money), in order to build or upgrade those roads that will bring the greatest net benefits.

In many contexts, it is also sensible for governments to decide how much to invest in resilience of a particular kind by doing a cost–benefit analysis in which the economic cost of disaster-scenarios (discounted by the risk of those scenarios arising) is compared with the economic cost of investing in resilience that would reduce the extent (and hence the economic cost) of the disaster. For events such as flooding, this kind of analysis is reasonably well established – and it provides a reasoned rebuttal to those who might otherwise claim that investment in resilience is a waste of money.

But in the case of unpredicted black-swan events causing serious persistent network failure, the supposed 'rationality' of traditional cost–benefit analysis breaks down – for several connected reasons.

In the first place, one can't assess the present value of the discounted economic cost of a society getting through a serious persistent network failure in any given year, unless one can estimate with reasonable assurance the probability of that particular type of network failure occurring in that particular year. And, as we have already seen, it is mind-numbingly difficult to lay hands on any method for determining such probabilities with any degree of assurance.

Second, one can't determine even the gross economic cost of a society getting through a network failure in vaguely reasonable shape without having a reasonable degree of assurance about the effects that the network failure will have on the society in question. One needs to be able to predict whether the effects will look and feel like the imaginary events portrayed in this book, or whether they will look and feel quite different (if, for example, the network failure is caused by a cyber-attack rather than a space-weather event). And it is difficult to predict this even a few years ahead, let alone many years hence, when all sorts of things will have changed in ways we can't yet imagine.

And, as if all of this weren't bad enough, there is another underlying problem: because distant events and low-probability events are both heavily discounted in any cost–benefit analysis, this form of calculation puts almost no weight on anything that might happen (but isn't likely to happen), say, three decades from now. A table in one of the clearest and most authoritative text-books on cost–benefit analysis, produced by the Stern

School of Business at New York University,[*] identifies one particular kind of risk, which it describes as 'Discontinuous market risk, with small likelihood of occurrence but large economic consequences' – i.e. exactly what one might call a black-swan event – and it goes on to give, as examples of such events, 'Political risk, Risk of expropriation, Terrorism risk', to which one might add 'serious persistent network failure'.

The textbook recommends 'risk adjustment in valuation' for these types of risk – telling us to allow for the cost of such risk in any investment calculation by including the 'cost of insurance' if 'insurance markets exist'.

But of course the textbook accepts that, in the case of true black-swan events such as systemic network failure, insurance markets are not likely to provide any insurance products to cover the economic loss. And, in this case, it advises the analyst appraising the investment simply to 'adjust the discount rate'.

So the analysts are, in effect, being advised to launch themselves headlong into the first of our three problems: they have no good way of ascertaining what the probability of the event is, and hence they have no good way of knowing how much to adjust the discount rate. But even

---

[*] Chapter 5 ('Risk Adjusted Value'), page 15. New York: Stern School of Business. http://people.stern.nyu.edu/adamodur/pdfiles/valrisk/ch5.pdf/

if they make a stab, and even if they assume that there is a relatively high probability of persistent and serious network failure, say 1%, then they have to arrive at a 'present value' that reflects the assumed 99% chance that the event won't occur in any given year.

Alas, even if they do this by multiplying the cost of the event by the probability of its occurrence before applying a discount for the time (instead of following the textbook's prescription to 'adjust the discount rate'), the effects of discounting the value of something that has a 99% chance of not happening thirty years from now are dramatic. Each million pounds of potential economic cost for society arising from a systemic network failure in year 30 would be assessed as having a present value of ($£1,000,000 \times 0.01)/(1.02^{30})$ or £5,500. In other words, the cost–benefit analysis would be telling you that it was worth spending only £5,500 today to guard against each £1 million of potential economic loss from network failure thirty years from now. And that is with an assessed probability of 1% that the event will happen in that year; with a probability of 0.1% or 0.01% (i.e. with chances of 1 in 1,000 or 1 in 10,000 of a given event happening thirty years from now, as is much more relevant to a black-swan event), then the calculated present value of protecting yourself against the effects of the potential event diminishes to £550 or £55 – i.e. effectively to zero.

For each of these three reasons – the difficulty of estimating probabilities, the difficulty of estimating economic benefits, and the very small value attributed in discounted cash-flow analysis to distant and improbable events – any application of cost–benefit analysis will lead either to the view that fallback-option strategies are not worth adopting or to the view that it is impossible to tell whether they are worth adopting. Therefore, if one remains as worried as I firmly believe we should be about the sort of events portrayed in the story told in this book, and as concerned as I think we should be to do things that will guard us against the worst effects of them, one has to throw cost–benefit analysis out of the window. (Incidentally, one is in good company here: cost–benefit analysis would certainly also have ruled out building the pyramids or Chartres Cathedral; there are more things in Heaven and Earth than are dreamt of in the philosophy of the business schools.)

I believe these arguments are intellectually compelling. But getting economically trained administrators to abandon traditional cost–benefit analysis is no easy matter. Setting out the intellectual case is not enough. Here, as in the case of the closely allied 'waste of money' argument, we need to apply emotional intelligence. We have to find a way of persuading administrators around the world, as a matter of intuition rather than calculation, that there are certain kinds of risk it is just not worth taking – at least if these risks can be avoided by providing cheap and cheerful 'make-do-and-mend' solutions that are well within our means.

My experience in government has persuaded me that the emotionally intelligent way of doing this is to *alter perspective by pinning responsibility*.

It is fairly easy for any administrator or politician in any government to look at risks like this and conclude that for 90 or 99% of the time (maybe even, if we are lucky, for 100% of the time) fallback options of the kind we are discussing will be totally useless – and will therefore appear totally unnecessary. There will be no shortage of people ready to point this out: newspapers, other politicians, other civil servants. Over and over again, all of these people will ask: why are we imposing these unnecessary costs on ourselves? Why should hard-pressed taxpayers be paying for measures from which they may never benefit? Is that fair?

And then, of course, if disaster does strike, the very same newspapers and politicians who were causing a fuss about the prospect of 'unnecessary expenditure unjustified by cost–benefit analysis' will instead be asking why no one took the necessary steps to provide the necessary fallback options.

The only way to persuade an administrator or politician to ignore such critics and concentrate on the risks is to make them *his or her risks*. If a particular politician or administrator in any government can be persuaded that, in the event of sustained catastrophic network failure, he or she will be directly in the firing line – that the newspapers and other politicians will be asking directly and individually why he or she hadn't created fallback options to get us through – then (as a matter of emotional intelligence rather than intellectual argument) that politician or administrator is likely to start concerning himself or herself with doing something about it. You can treat huge problems as other people's problems only for so long as they don't become your problem.

Interestingly at present no government (of which I am aware) clearly identifies a specific individual who is responsible for dealing with serious persistent network failure. Of course, in any government, responsibility for everything is to some extent diffused because modern governments everywhere in the world are large and complicated. But, in most modern governments, you can nevertheless find out pretty easily who is responsible for education or welfare or defence – at least so far as day-to-day base-level operations are concerned. By contrast, if you try to discover who is responsible for enabling any nation to get through serious persistent network failure, you will find yourself engaged in a long research project with no very definite conclusion. In the UK (which is among the world leaders in this area), responsibility is 'shared' between the National Security Council; the Cabinet Office; the Treasury; the Home Office; the Department for Business, Energy and Industrial Strategy; the Department for Digital, Culture, Media and Sport; the Ministry of Defence; the Department for Transport; the Department for Environment, Food and Rural Affairs (Defra); the Bank of England; GCHQ (and the National Cyber Centre); Ofcom; Ofwat; Ofgem; and National Grid. That is quite enough people for each to be able to blame the others if and when disaster strikes. So no one feels that it will be their own neck on the chopping-block.

It is something of a miracle that, despite this diffusion of responsibility, the Cabinet Office has taken the matter in hand in the UK. There can be absolutely no guarantee – or even presumption – that this will go on being true in subsequent administrations. And it is no surprise that, in many countries, the diffusion of responsibility has been associated with what has every appearance of inaction. To raise the stakes, to bring home the risks, and to defeat the intellectually defunct critique from the cost–benefit merchants, this issue needs to become the direct responsibility of an individual person within government who has the power to make things happen, and who knows that their own reputation is directly on the line. That is the way to concentrate minds.

▲

Being aware of dependency

But concentrating minds on finding solutions will work only if the minds in question have also become fully aware of the extent of the problem.

Part of the purpose of the story in this book is to illustrate more vividly the factual point made in earlier analytical chapters – that we are all becoming inevitably and increasingly dependent on converging technologies and hence on the converging networks that support those technologies. But there aren't yet very many people, inside or outside governments, who are vividly aware of these dependencies. As I have mentioned, one now finds an expert or two at any relevant seminar who is seriously worried, and that is a start. But it is a long way from this becoming something that governments and business leaders take really seriously, in the way they do other long-term challenges such as unemployment, social care or the health service, or air pollution and climate change.

So, just as there is a communications challenge when it comes to alerting the media and the voting public to the extent of the vulnerability, there is also the internal communications challenge of making politicians and administrators sufficiently aware of the problem.

My guess is that, in most countries, the route to achieving this is via the military. It is the military who specialize in thinking about threats that are distant and not very likely to arise, but which are so worrying that we need to be defended against them: most military risks are like this. It is also the military who specialize in making plans: when I was working in government, I frequently found that the defence establishment had made plans for things that were extraordinarily unlikely to occur, whereas the civilian departments often had no adequate plans to deal with things that were very likely indeed to occur. This comes about partly because the military are geared up to make plans to deal with low-probability risks: they have planning teams, planning tools, planning specialists and so forth. It also comes about partly because a large part of the military personnel in any country are not usually engaged in fighting, so they spend their time training and planning, whereas civilian departments in any government are continuously operating on the front-line – legislating, regulating, litigating, negotiating, providing public services and so forth – and therefore don't have much time for planning, especially in relation to low-probability risks. It should therefore be relatively easy in most countries to interest the military in the idea of understanding the extent to which our network-dependency makes us vulnerable, and in the idea of planning how to deal with that vulnerability.

But there is another reason for starting with the military. When one is trying to alert politicians and administrators to the scale of low-probability, high-impact black-swan events, one of the challenges is just to get in the door – to get the issue taken seriously. And one of the things that gets you in the door is the military because you can't dismiss them as zany or childlike. They are very obviously grown up.

What is more, the military tend to have the invaluable characteristic of longevity. They build up what they call 'doctrine' and they hand it on from one generation to the next. So, once they build a given kind of risk or threat into their planning, and build a 'doctrine' around it, they keep this in existence for many years, and keep coming back to it. In the case of network-dependency risks, this is hugely helpful, since it increases the chance of ensuring that successive civilian politicians and administrators will be alerted to the problem and will come to regard it as 'something on the agenda', rather than as something too difficult and too distant to worry about.

Of course, in liberal democracies the military are not in charge. Convincing them that network-dependency creates risks to which we should be fully and continuously alive is not in itself sufficient. It is just the start – and there will be a long slog before the military can convince others in succeeding administrations to take these risks seriously. But it is a good way in.

And I don't believe it should be particularly difficult to persuade the military in most countries to take this seriously – not least because, from a military point of view, it is so blindingly obvious that, if you wanted to paralyse an enemy and make them vulnerable, you couldn't do better than to deprive them of the networks that they use for energy, communications and transport. The emergence of cyber-warfare alone serves to illustrate very clearly the growing significance of networks in the defence/offence equation. It doesn't take much imagination to see that what applies to communications networks in a cyber-age, applies also increasingly (and increasingly connectedly) to energy and transport networks. So the military need only think of what attacks they might successfully launch against the networks of others, to see how important it is for us (whoever 'we' may be) to prevent others (or indeed nature) sending attacks of the same sort our way.

But I think one can, in fact, go further than this. One can say with some confidence that network-vulnerability is fast becoming one of the main issues in defence.

Recent events in the Middle East have illustrated vividly the difficulties and dangers of invasion under twenty-first-century conditions, even where the invader ostensibly has overwhelming force at its disposal. And, with the possible and worrying exception of North Korea, there is now widespread understanding of the horrors associated with a thermo-nuclear attack. This leaves only one form of threat that minimizes risks for the aggressor and yet also has the capacity to render the recipient almost as helpless as a highly focused neutron bomb:

namely, an attack on the networks on which the recipient nation depends. Indeed, the consequences of such an
attack are likely to be so damaging that even the credible
threat of carrying one out may be enough to act as a
powerful form of blackmail, enabling the aggressor to
achieve its ends without the need to bring down the
adversary's networks in a serious and persistent way. To
any power with the relevant offensive technology, this is
aggressive warfare almost for free. Accordingly, in defence
terms, the chance that another country, or some highly
sophisticated non-state actor, will in the not too distant
future attempt to put a metaphorical gun to our heads
by threatening the integrity of our core networks is high
enough to raise concern among the military.

For all of these reasons, engaging the military is
the obvious way of fostering a heightened awareness of
network-dependency across the whole of government.

Recalling the recent past

But even if the military do become strong advocates of
the need to worry about network-dependency, there is
likely to be resistance of a different type from government
departments.

Paradoxically, this other type of resistance arises from
the assumption that the core networks have become so
fundamental a part of our lives as to be irreplaceable.

Many people within government establishments across the world are so impressed by the power of modern networks that they find it inconceivable for such networks to be substituted, even for a few days, by cheap and cheerful 'make-do-and-mend' fallback options.

It is entirely understandable that the assumption of irreplaceability often prevents people from believing in the possibility of cheap replacements. We are becoming so impressed by the capacities of modern, network-based technologies, and so dependent on them, that anything less can easily seem unimaginable. This is just another symptom of the fundamental problem that the whole architecture of our lives is now increasingly constructed on the foundations laid by modern networks. But there is nevertheless an obvious and convincing riposte to the argument that no cheaper and simpler fallback option is possible – namely, that simpler, cheaper and less capable systems did exist in the recent past, so they must be possible. We now depend, for example, on smartphones and a wide range of electronic communications. But it wasn't very long ago that these things were a matter of science fiction and futurology. It really is true that we once (in fact, just a few years ago) used phones only for voice communications; all written communication was by post, telex or telegraph. So it is possible to imagine getting by with phones that just do voice communications. If we did it a few years back, we could do it now.

What is remarkable is that we have so little inclination to consider the recent past as a source of ideas
about what to do if circumstances in the present rob us of
recent advances. We are all trained so well to think about
progress and new technological frontiers – as we generally
should – that we have almost lost the knack of winding
back the clock a little when events take a turn that makes
it rational to do so. This is a knack that we need to regain
if we are to devise sensible fallback options to deal with
episodes of sustained catastrophic network failure. The
recent past is a treasure house of the definitively practical
– which doesn't need deep research or bold experiment,
but can simply be brought back into use as a fail-safe fallback if more modern technologies go wrong.

The trick, of course, is to go far enough back without
going too far back. We should search for fallback options
which are from a sufficiently distant past to enable them
to be genuinely stand-alone (i.e. not in any way dependent
on the modern networks they will be used to replace in an
emergency); but which are from a sufficiently near past to
be as efficient as possible when they are used. To return
to the example of communications, voice-only mobile
technology is preferable to carrier-pigeons as a replacement for smartphones if, but only if, it can function
without using the networks that have been taken down
by whatever attack has occurred. If it turns out that voice
networks will inevitably be dependent on the networks

that we are aiming to replace in an emergency, then we should go back a generation or two to search for the most recent technology that isn't ruled out by such dependence – even then, if possible, avoiding technologies from the distant past like carrier-pigeons.

In short, by working back from the present, through layers of the recent and then less recent technologies, we can reasonably hope to identify optimal fallback options. And this is exactly the kind of thinking that we need to engender in administrations around the world if we are to reduce the vulnerability of mankind to attacks that cause persistent, serious failure of the ultra-modern networks on which we currently depend in normal circumstances.

Admitting that things could go wrong

But bureaucracies need to get through another pain-barrier before they will contemplate sponsoring second-best fallback solutions even from the recent past.

The pain-barrier in question is the horror of admitting that all the defences that have been carefully and expensively constructed to protect the modern networks on which we normally depend really might fail.

The paradox here is that the more expert and the more serious a particular government (or indeed, a particular industry) becomes about constructing network defences, the more hideous the pain of admitting the possibility of failure. It's like children with sand-castles: the family that hastily throws together a motte-and-bailey castle out of a single bucket and a piece of driftwood will be able to accept with equanimity the moment when the tide washes the ramshackle construction away, whereas the family that has spent hours constructing a magnificent Krak des Chevaliers among sand-castles, complete with succeeding lines of carefully crenelated defensive walls, will be loathe to entertain the notion that the whole thing may be demolished in a trice by the overwhelming power of the sea.

This is not to decry efforts to construct serious defences for modern networks. On the contrary, the economic and social value of the network technologies on which we now normally depend is so great that it is well worth investing large amounts of time and effort in defending them against all forms of attack (both natural and human) to which they are likely to be subject: the sand-castles should indeed be crenelated Kraks des Chevaliers. But the more effort we put into this necessary task and the more splendid our network defences become, the more trouble we need to take to prevent the possibility of failure disappearing from view.

There are various ways in which governments and businesses can guard against losing sight of the possibility of failure. The most obvious method is to separate clearly between 'green' and 'red' teams: a 'green' team in charge of building, maintaining and updating the defences, and a completely separate 'red' team in charge of working out what fallback options need to be in place in case the defences fail. By doing this, the administration as a whole can avoid suffering the otherwise almost inevitable psychological consequences of a commitment to superior defence. The 'green' team committed to constructing defence doesn't need to entertain the terrible thought of failure, because their separate colleagues in the 'red' team relieve them of that obligation. Each team can focus wholeheartedly on its particular aim, without being psychologically torn.

Such bureaucratic structures do not, however, guarantee that the most senior figures in any administration will overcome the fear of admitting that the defences may fail. This is because senior figures cannot easily be restricted to operating as part of a 'green' or 'red' team – and there are considerable incentives for any senior minister who is not solely concerned with constructing fallback options to avoid confronting the awful truth that the government of which he or she is a prominent part may find that all the network defences in which it has invested huge amounts of time and money could actually fail. Any such admission risks the headline: 'Minister admits security flop', closely followed by an article confidently telling readers that 'In an astonishingly frank admission, minister X today conceded that the billions spent on defending key networks may actually fail to preserve normal operation under attack conditions.' Of course, in any rational world, the minister would go on to explain that this was merely an inevitable fact, since no defence, however elaborate, well planned and well funded, can possibly be perfect. But the media circus that surrounds governments and large businesses is not rational; it sweeps people and arguments along in a great tide of emotion, and the losers are people who have long, rational answers to short, irrational questions. Senior figures in any government are well aware of this and are therefore naturally reluctant to indulge in speculation about failed defences and fallback options.

The way out of this bind is for governments to seize the initiative at times when there is no crisis and not even any whiff of crises to come. By proactively announcing that fallback options are being added to investment in defence, and by describing this as a 'second-line of protection for the economy and society', ministers can protect themselves against lurid accusations of defeatism and panic, and can instead (accurately) represent the recognition of the possibility that the first (defensive) line of protection may fail as a strength rather than a weakness of their approach. By acting in this way, they can also create sufficient public understanding of fallback options to avoid damaging and inaccurate media stories later about 'secret plans to deal with expected network failure': plans that are announced cannot be secret, and what is not secret is not much of a story.

From probability to scenario analysis

Once a 'red' team has been established to look at fallback options to cover failure while the 'green' team works on improving network defences to prevent failure, the 'red' team needs to adopt a method of working that is wholly different from the way the 'green' team works.

When you are designing and building defences to protect modern networks, you need to start with probability analysis – because you can't afford to protect the networks against every conceivable form of attack, and it therefore makes sense to protect them against the most likely forms of attack. Of course, the 'green' team needs to be conscious of all the points about misleading statistics that were made in earlier chapters of this book; but the fact remains that statistics – and the assessment of probability that statistics make possible – are an invaluable part of the 'green' team's equipment.

By contrast, the 'red' team, which is designing fallback options to be used if there is network failure, should *totally avoid any reference to statistics and probabilities*. It should focus remorselessly on worst-case scenarios, without worrying in the least about how likely these are to occur. This ought to be obvious – but it will seem quite counter-intuitive in any established bureaucracy, because established bureaucracies are used not only to cost–benefit analysis of the sort that is so destructive of fallback-option planning but also to the allied pursuit of probability analysis. It becomes a habit in any well-trained bureaucracy to consider probabilities before taking action. But the 'red' team has to overcome this habit. It has to recognize that the whole point of fallback-option planning is to quit worrying about how likely it is that network failure of any particular kind will occur for any particular reason, and to concentrate instead on how to make society and the economy capable of carrying on in a half-way reasonable fashion if and when network failure does occur. So probabilities don't matter to the 'red' team doing the work on fallback options. What should matter to this team is only the ability of the state and society to handle serious persistent network failure in a reasonably robust way.

Another way of putting this is that the 'red' team doing the fallback-option planning needs to use scenario analysis instead of probability analysis.

It is worth emphasizing this point, because serious scenario analysis is unusual in any government, and involves habits of mind that are not frequently found outside the military. It is fairly straightforward to slap down on a piece of paper a broad scenario, and then proceed without much further analysis to construct a fallback option that will apply in the event that this scenario becomes real. But serious scenario analysis involves much more than this. It means working through the ramifications and consequences of the scenario – understanding the full range of what is likely to go wrong if modern convergent networks fail. And this includes not just administrative issues but also the human dimension – the effects on people who are living through the network failure. In other words, it means constructing stories like the story told in this book, and then thinking through how to enable people to live through such stories in a way that gives the story a different and better ending. That is a work of imagination which will not come naturally to any bureaucracy that is attuned to considering systems and statistics rather than stories and human consequences.

The value of trial and error

This need for the 'red' team to step outside the normal, bureaucratic mind-set when analysing scenarios is closely allied to another unusual requirement for successful fallback-option planning: a willingness to proceed on the basis of trial and error.

Because fallback options are by definition not the way we go about our business most of the time in our ordinary lives, they can't be refined through the experience gained from daily use, in the way that is now usual with the evolution of modern networks. But there is one strategic advantage on which administrators building fallback options can rely: namely, that they have time on their hands. With any luck, the serious persistent network failures that could cause us to use the fallback options will not happen soon, if they happen at all. So the fallback-option planners can do things in less of a rush than is often the case in government or in commerce. Instead of the remorseless pressure that is imposed on democratic governments by the news cycle and the electoral cycle, or the remorseless pressure imposed by competition on businesses, the fallback-option planners can operate in a quiet bubble and do their planning without very much notice being taken of it by anyone outside government. As a consequence, they can take the time to get it right by trying things out on a relatively small scale to see whether they work before they roll them out on a wider scale. In other words, they can use trial and error, without much risk of being heavily castigated in public either for being too slow or for making errors along the way.

This, too, will be counter-intuitive for most bureaucracies and most politicians in most countries. They are used to operating under pressures that make trial and error a dangerous approach; so they learn to do a huge amount of analysis and then to introduce change in one Big Bang – claiming, however implausibly, that the change is perfect. They live in hope that the change will either turn out to be such a success that any minor imperfections will be overlooked, or that the true effects of the change will not become evident while they are still in post.

Whether, given all the pressures on politicians and administrators, this 'analyse and change' approach is actually a sensible way of implementing public policy in general is an interesting and open question. But the one thing we can be sure of is that it will be less likely to produce respectable results than the trial and error approach, which we tend to use in our own lives. So the ability to use trial and error in order to build up, patiently, a set of workable fallback options behind the veil of relative public obscurity is a luxury that administrators need to be persuaded to take full advantage of.

There is, of course, a close connection between the use of such trial and error techniques and the reliance that fallback-option planning needs to place on scenarios rather than statistics. By imagining worst-case scenarios, and then testing small-scale fallback-option experiments against enactments of these scenarios, fallback-option planners can accumulate true empirical information about what works and what doesn't – and can then roll out only those fallback options that have been shown to work in a wide range of extreme scenarios.

Evidently, this kind of trial and error testing will never guarantee success, because one can never guarantee that even a 'red' team devoted wholly to the task will identify all of the scenarios that actually come to pass or all of the relevant features of those scenarios. But at least the development of fallback options can be an example of public policy produced and tested with as much rigour and patience as is applied in research science or in life-and-death settings such as drug development and military planning. This is much more than can be said of most public policy.

Experts

There is, however, one final element required for the development of suitable fallback options. This is the identification of the right people to be the experts on whom the 'red' team can rely when they are doing their work.

It is much easier to spot this need than to fulfil it.

In many areas of public policy, there are easily identified professional experts. Here, there is no profession – and the kinds of expertise required are enormously varied. Naturally, the work requires a full understanding of a wide range of modern convergent technologies and networks. But it also requires an intimate knowledge of the way that these networks and technologies are used by a plethora of different people in a plethora of different activities, as well as a deep understanding of the potential for the continuation of these activities with technologies from the recent past, to which we might plausibly fall back in a case of sustained catastrophic network failure.

Assembling a team of people with all of these skills is not easy. What makes this challenge even greater than it would otherwise be is that the natural tendency of bureaucracies when faced with complex problems – to employ huge numbers of people with differing skills and knowledge – won't work very well in this case. As all of the features of any fallback option will be connected with one another, they will need to be considered simultaneously or iteratively rather than in series; this means that a small team, which can discuss the challenges informally and repeatedly in the round, rather than becoming an unwieldy bureaucracy in itself, is far preferable to a large mass of administrators and experts. So the best solution is a narrow group of people with a wide assembly of knowledge: creating that is no mean feat. No doubt, this is one of the reasons why fallback options are so rare – and hence one of the reasons why the events in our story are so likely to be played out somewhere in the future.

8

FOR WHOM THE BELL TOLLS

The remainder of Bill Donoghue's New Year's Day – the return to East Coker; the efforts (eventually successful) to persuade Mary to come with him; the long drive through the afternoon, retracing his steps along the A30 into London; dropping Mary at his flat in Broadgate (by now seemingly as cold inside as it was outside); finding some cold food for both of them in the temporarily defunct fridge and a torch for each of them; trying to make sure she was wrapped up as warmly as he could manage; the return to the Bank; the rather garbled explanations from the door-keeper there about the repeated efforts by the military to track him down – all of this was a merciful blur in his mind as he made his way over to the 10 p.m. COBR meeting at the Cabinet Office in an army Land Rover.

As none of the communications at the Bank were functioning, he knew no more than when he had first left the building twenty-one hours previously. So he couldn't bring any up-to-date information to the COBR meeting. But he had at least got a basic run-down on the general situation from the young lieutenant-colonel who had been sent to collect him, and he could patch together some thoughts about what was likely to happen to global financial markets the next day if London was still a black hole by then. Presumably, that was what they would really want to know from him.

He entered the room and found the place at the table marked 'Bank of England' just before the PM came in and opened the meeting.

'Thank you all for coming. I need hardly remind you that it is now exactly twelve hours since we were last in this room. I am grateful to those who have been working hard over those twelve hours to deal with the situation.

'I want to begin with the grid. Charles: could you give us a status report please?'

For Charles Hoare, the young Business and Energy Secretary, this was a baptism of fire. A farmer by profession, he had been moved the previous September from a Minister of State job at the Department for Environment, Food and Rural Affairs where he had felt entirely at home, to this new department about which he knew nothing. It had been his intention to look into the resilience of the energy system at some point, but learning about the everyday business involved in his vast new portfolio had taken all his time, and he had acquired only the sketchiest understanding of how the energy system worked. However, now was not a moment to admit ignorance.

'Well, Prime Minister, with the help of the military, my private office have established a direct – though somewhat primitive – communications link with National Grid. I last received a report from the grid at 9 p.m., in preparation for this COBR meeting. The details are complicated, but the essence is that the work on restoring power following the grid failure has begun. A black start has been successfully conducted at two southern power stations. And the integrity of the grid and distribution network has been investigated in the area surrounding each of those stations. Power has therefore been restored in two small areas covering, between them, about 300,000 premises. From this point onwards, larger pools of light will be created as the night progresses – though, as I know you are already aware, the balancing of the system will at various stages require some areas where power has been restored to be blacked out temporarily before coming back into permanent operation. National Grid has not yet found examples of large-scale permanent damage to transformers or other equipment, and therefore remains hopeful that full power will be restored across the country by some time on 5 January.'

So that, at least, was progressing as expected. The next question was the elderly. 'Thank you, Charles. I now want to turn to you, CDS. How far have we got with establishing a command and control system for the adult social services and NHS emergency services?'

The Chief of the Defence Staff, Andrew Ark, had spent the previous hour with the Defence Secretary working out how to answer this inevitable question. They had decided that the best solution was honesty. But they didn't expect this to be an easy ride:

'Prime Minister, I'm afraid the news on that front is not good. The senior staff responsible for civil emergencies at almost all first-tier local authorities have come into their offices despite it being New Year's Day; their reserve generators have kicked in; and their computers are functioning. I have officers present in the central headquarters of each county and city council. But the council computers have no access to the cloud, and no other means of communicating apart from our army radio system. The result is that they have no access to any data file that would give the physical locations of any of the agencies running the social care in their area, or of any council staff involved in direct provision of care. What is worse, I see no prospect of this situation changing until power and communications are restored in a given area. At that point, of course, the councils will be able to locate the agencies; but, by that time, our military system will no longer be required. In the meantime, I have a resource, but I have no way of deploying it to create an effective command and control system. I am therefore putting all military effort into establishing, with the local civil emergency staff, holding centres at locations in each town or borough which can be provided with light, heat and food – with arrangements for military couriers to shuttle as necessary between these centres and hospitals in order to mobilize ambulances. We will have to rely on relatives, friends and care workers to make their way into these centres, or into council headquarters, from which they can be directed to the centres.'

So it was as bad as the PM had imagined. No prior plan. Not even a back-up database in each council. The whole system depended on the flawed assumption that everyone could rely on the availability of cloud-computing and normal communications. And the worst of it was that the person ultimately responsible for this complete failure of resilience planning was him; he was, after all, the Prime Minister.

'So what you are telling me, CDS, is that we just have to hope, over the next four days, that individual care workers, relatives and friends are going to identify those frail, elderly people who are in need, and that they are going to find some means either of looking after them or of bringing them to centres of whose existence they are currently unaware.'

Andrew Ark found himself admiring the PM's command of syntax in a crisis. But he had no comfort to offer.

'Yes, Prime Minister. That is an accurate summary of the situation.'

The meeting dragged on for another forty-five min- utes, as they combed through the weather forecast, the transport situation, the position in the hospitals, the likely events as some workers turned up to offices and factories in the morning, the reaction of the public to the fact that they wouldn't be able to buy anything even if the shops opened, the possibility that people in some places would attempt to steal what they couldn't buy or beg . . . on and on through an accumulating series of problems to which there were no solutions, or rather to all of which there was just the one solution of restoring the energy and communications systems by getting the grid up and running again.

Just as things were drawing to a close, Bill realized with a start that the Chancellor of the Exchequer, Jane Baldwin, was referring to him: 'On the question you have raised about the effect on global markets, Prime Minister, I think Dr Donoghue from the Bank of England is best placed to answer.'

Bill wasn't sure of the etiquette. Should he wait to be asked, or just chip in? He decided that the PM would probably appreciate some proactivity: 'Yes, Chancellor, as all global markets have been closed for the last twenty-four hours or so, and as our communications at the Bank have been closed off like everyone else's' (in his exhausted state he was tempted to add, but didn't, 'and as I have been looking after my mother-in-law in Somerset'), 'I have no actual information to report. But I can describe what is likely to happen over the next few days, if that would be helpful.'

'Thank you. We would certainly like to hear that.'

'We start with one piece of luck. Because the comms black-out started at a time when the markets were closed, we do not have the nightmare prospect that we would have had if we had been in the middle of a trading day – when millions, maybe billions of transactions would have been left incomplete, possibly causing years of effort to unpick and provide redress for those who had incurred losses. However, we have a different problem. London is a vast network of interlocking global markets. Many of these involve transactions that are originated elsewhere in the world and are controlled by complex software rather than being generated by human action. So, for example, the margin payments on over-the-counter derivatives such as credit default swaps through the London clearing houses are made automatically by the relevant software, much of which will be located in servers held elsewhere in the world. When the packages of data sent out by all of these servers attempt to find routes through the global network to the relevant server in London, they will be bounced back. This will generate automatic attempts by the software to find other routes, thereby multiplying indefinitely the amount of traffic seeking a home on global networks. It is extremely difficult to predict the total effect, which will depend on the density of failed transactions in the first hours and the speed with which human intervention can be used to close down programs that are generating impossible transactions. But my personal guess, having considered this in the past, is that the global networks are likely to become inoperable over the course of the next day or so.'

This was a new dimension of which the PM had had no previous inkling. His eyes widened. 'I'm sorry, Dr Donoghue. This is all new to me. Are you telling us that the whole world's communications systems are likely to be brought down by what is happening in London?'

'Yes, Prime Minister. That is my broad conclusion. This will, in turn, ricochet into the operation of other financial markets and into the operation of the energy, transport and commercial credit markets in real economies around the world. The extent to which particular economies or societies are able to support simple transactions like buying and selling food will, of course, depend on the extent of sophistication and convergence in those economies and the extent of the fallback systems, if any, that have been installed. My guess is that this will be a case in which the least developed countries fare far better than the most developed. In large parts of sub-Saharan Africa, for example, life may continue pretty much as normal. I

doubt that this will be true of the richer northern countries, or indeed of most of Asia, which is now thoroughly
linked into global networks and has leap-frogged into
technologies, if anything, more convergent than our own.'

So they were dealing with what could well become a
global rather than merely a national crisis – if, of course,
it wasn't one already. And the PM was at risk of being
blamed not just for what happened to his own people
but to the whole world. Strangest of all, there was no way
he could communicate these facts to his counterparts
elsewhere across the globe. It was like being an active
mind locked in a body that would not allow any speech
or gestures.

Come to think of it, he should check that: 'Defence
Secretary, can you or the Transport Secretary give us any
insight into the possibility of sending information by air
to other parts of the world – or even by terrestrial transport to the continent?'

Harold Stuart, conscious that the reputation of the
Ministry of Defence had not been enhanced by the total
failure to implement a plan of the sort that the Chief of
the Defence Staff had proposed for social care just twelve
hours previously, was keen to move back into 'can do'
mode.

'Yes, Prime Minister, the Transport Secretary and I
have discussed exactly that. Normal civilian flights will
not be feasible. It will probably take about three days

before the GPS systems are fully operational again, even assuming that none of the satellites have been permanently damaged; all airports will be operating only on back-up generation, which is not sufficient to maintain normal passenger services. Our guess, though we haven't been able to confirm it yet, is that the airline reservation system will have gone down with the Internet, as it is all now IP-based; and there are question marks over the possibility that the magnetic impulse from the space-weather event may have residual effects on avionics, which will probably make the Civil Aviation Authority reluctant to authorize any flights, though we haven't yet been able to contact anyone there. I am told that we could in theory use military aircraft with in-flight refuelling as necessary to reach at least a small number of key overseas destinations, using more traditional navigation techniques that don't rely on satellite navigation systems. But we are very concerned that, without any prior ground-to-ground communication, military aircraft entering foreign airspace may be refused permission to land. So my conclusion is that we should aim at immediate despatch of small vessels to selected ports across the Channel in the hope of identifying at least one location where the space-weather event has not had anything like the effect it has had in the UK, and from which communication could be established with the rest of the world before the start of play tomorrow. Simultaneously, my team has been trying to identify anyone either inside the military or in the amateur radio ham community who is still using old-fashioned high-frequency 1.8 MHz to 28 MHz transceivers that either rely on the old 13.8 volt batteries or could be run off power from army generators to establish contact with radio ham counterparts or military counterparts in other 'five-eyes' countries* or in Europe. As these remain completely outside the Internet, they are likely to have been (and to remain) unaffected by the paralysis of the normal comms systems. Perhaps I could discuss with you and the Foreign Secretary directly after this meeting which destinations we should choose, and what messages we should send?'

The Prime Minister glimpsed one flickering beacon of light in the darkness.

He wanted to quit while he was ahead: 'Thank you, Harold. Let's do just that. Jane, I think you should join Liz and myself for that conversation. We will meet again in COBR at 10 a.m. tomorrow.'

▲

As Bill Donoghue made his way back to the Bank, he found himself amazed at the prediction he had just made. Would the whole world's financial and communications

---

* The five-eyes countries are Australia, Canada, New Zealand, the UK and the USA; they are bound by a treaty for joint cooperation in signals intelligence.

systems *really* come crashing down? And how on earth would they put the pieces back together again if they did?

When he reached the inner courtyard, he made his way up towards the Governor's parlour in the hope that the army might by now have made contact with the Governor, or that the Governor might have come in on his own initiative. No such luck. Presumably, the army had decided that one representative from the Bank was enough for COBR; and the Governor might well have been unable to make the journey from his holiday in the Caribbean, even by military plane.

Bill couldn't see any useful purpose to remaining in his office overnight. His screens were still dead, which meant that he wouldn't learn anything new even when the Asian markets opened in the next few hours – if, indeed, they did open. He made arrangements with the door-keeper to pass on the message that he would be back at 7 a.m., ready to do anything it turned out to be possible to do before setting off for the COBR meeting at 9, and then left for Broadgate.

He was entirely unprepared for the scene that greeted him when he had climbed the six flights of stairs from the basement garage to his flat on the fifth floor, lighting his way with his torch. Mary Hughes, whom he had expected to find tucked up in bed beneath the many layers of blankets with which he had so carefully surrounded her, was instead sitting, covered in some of the same blankets, on one of the arm chairs in the main room. God knows how long she had been there. As he touched her shoulder and spoke to her, he began to think of the various possible explanations. But he didn't need to speculate, as she woke almost immediately from her slumber. She quickly made him understand that she was sitting upright because – perhaps shocked by the cold when getting out of bed – she had fallen against the door of the bathroom, and had hit the back of her rib-cage, which was now too sore to let her sleep when lying down. She looked horribly pale, and admitted to him that she had vomited not long before he arrived home. He clearly needed to get her to Guy's Hospital for a check-up. But how to get her downstairs when the lift was out of operation?

He decided there was nothing for it but to cradle her in his arms and to make his way down with her, clutching the stair rail as firmly as he could to stop himself falling. By comparison, the drive to A&E at Guy's, where he managed to find one of the idle ambulance staff to help her into the reception area, was easy. But he realized as soon as he got inside that getting her seen by someone was going to be anything but easy. The whole place was jammed with people, most of them ostensibly in a similar position to his own – distressed, elderly folk accompanied by middle-aged friends or relatives. The ticket for 'triage' that he received from the machine by the door showed a number 171 greater than was showing on the digital sign for 'next patient'. If that was the queue for triage, it was going to take an eternity, and probably more, even to get to that stage, let alone the time they would then have to spend waiting for the full diagnostics, once the triage medic had decided such diagnosis was needed (as he was sure they would).

He needn't have worried, on that score at least – because, from that moment, things moved into fast motion. Mary's vomiting began again, and she was rushed into intensive care. In the nightmarish blur that followed, one episode seemed to meld seamlessly into the next: hurried conversations with one of the doctors; a dash to some kind of scanning machine; references to a punctured lung; blood in profusion as another machine was used to drain the lung; Mary, all the while, looking paler and frailer; eventually, with seeming inevitability, the oxygen mask; the death rattle, which even he recognized; the anxious faces of the medics around him; and she was gone. She was 150 miles from her daughter, and he had no means even of conveying the news to Elaine. Bill felt winded and a little nauseous. Was it his fault? Should he have done something different? He knew that he would never know, and that he would never quite be at peace, not knowing.

The paperwork dragged on for ever. It seemed unimaginable that, in the midst of this crisis and chaos, the bureaucracy still demanded the forms to be filled in. By the time he reached his car, it was 05:35. Just early enough to get back to the flat to wash and change before going back into the Bank.

▲

The mood at the 10 a.m. COBR meeting was subdued. This was the fourth discussion since the beginning of the crisis; thirty-four hours after the moment when Britain had shut down. It was a Saturday, and therefore the first true working day was not until Monday. But there was still no sign of electricity or communications. Nobody was able to shop or cook or recharge their cars or use the motorways. Deep cold had set into every home in the country, apart from the houses lucky enough to have a log fire.

For Bill, that meeting and its five successors over the remainder of the weekend formed one long sequence of surreal events, permeated by the misery and anxiety of being unable to see or communicate with Elaine when he most needed her and she most needed to hear from him. In retrospect, he wasn't able to pinpoint with any precision the meeting at which it was reported that contact had been established with administrations abroad, first via a ship sent to France and thereafter via ham-radio directly from the UK, or the times when reports came in of the gradually increasing 'pools of light' as the National Grid was restored – exactly as predicted by Jan Sikorski.

But he could precisely recall that, just before setting off for the 10 a.m. COBR meeting on Monday 4 January, his screens at the Bank had come back to life; the phones had started working again; life was clearly returning to something much closer to normal. As the participants gathered in 70 Whitehall, everyone had the same story to tell. The immediate crisis was close to over. But what was the reckoning? How many other families had suffered losses like his own? Or worse?

For the PM, this was in many ways the most difficult moment of all. Up until now, his attention had been focused on tackling the emergency – setting up warm centres manned by the military to shelter the elderly and distribute food; communicating with the rest of the world; above all, restoring power and mass communications at home. But now that things were normalizing, he was going to have to do something much more personal. With broadcasting restored and the rest of the media back in operation, he was going to have to explain to Parliament and to the people what had happened and why it had been allowed to happen.

He knew that there was no point in asking anyone else in the room for sympathy. Like him, most of them had been working with ridiculously little sleep for 120 hours; like him, they had been focusing on the job at hand, hugely exerting, but mercifully impersonal; now, they too would be worrying about their own personal shares of responsibility. To the extent that they were concerned about him, the issue in their minds would not be his coming ordeal. Rather, it would be whether he would turn them into fall-guys or how, if he himself went, they would be treated by his successor.

He must therefore be strictly business-like.

'I am very grateful for all the work that has been done by you, Charles, and colleagues at National Grid to restore power. I will turn to the other services later in this meeting. But I think we should begin with a report from the Health Secretary and the Local Government Secretary. Frank: what can you and Eric tell us about the numbers of frail, elderly people that have been affected?'

'Prime Minister, we have now established communication with almost all hospitals, and Eric's colleagues will be working through today to communicate with primary local authorities about the social care system. I am also very grateful to Harold and to the CDS for the continuous reports we have received via the military and their safe-centres. I'm afraid that the information, while incomplete at this stage, is not encouraging. All hospitals report large numbers of elderly patients who are either critically ill or have died. Despite the low levels of elective surgery over the New Year period and the consequent availability of beds, all hospitals also report massive overcrowding. Many have numbers exceeding even the available trolleys.'

So there were elderly patients lying on hospital floors.

The PM had suspected as much. It was going to be impossible to find any way of excusing that. 'Can you be any more precise? Are we talking about thousands or tens of thousands of deaths?'

'Well, Prime Minister, I don't want to give you precise numbers when we don't have any. But, anecdotally, my impression is that we are talking about very large numbers. Given the number of frail, elderly people normally receiving care at home, and even allowing for the help that many will have been receiving from relatives or neighbours, we would still be talking about just less than 400,000 people at risk from the cold and from shortage of food. It would be a miracle if more than three-quarters of those have come through unharmed. Looked at another way, we have about 150 major hospitals of varying sizes; direct Department of Health contacts with them, which began early this morning, combined with the military reports that have been coming in since Thursday, suggest that the larger hospitals have been dealing with thousands rather than hundreds of cases each, and that the death-rates among these patients have been alarmingly high.

'We then have to guess what fraction of the frail, elderly people who needed to go to hospital or to a military safe-centre have been unable to do so, due to their own inability to communicate during these days and the lack of anyone from the outside being able to get to them. Your guess is as good as mine at this stage, but I'd be amazed if there aren't tens of thousands in that category too. Given what we have seen in the hospitals, I would expect a very high proportion of those unable to reach A&E to have died or to be in a critical condition. All in all, I would say that the number of people dying who would otherwise not have died over this period will probably be nearer a hundred thousand than ten thousand.'

A horrified silence settled on the room. It was absolutely as bad as the PM had come to expect. Ever since those first two COBRs, at which it had become evident that the army could establish safe-centres and could provide transport to them but couldn't provide any serious organization for the 0.75 million domiciliary care workers, he had assumed that the worst consequence of this disaster would be deaths among the frail elderly. Now, that was being confirmed. Neither Parliament nor the media would forgive him. The sense of foreboding with which he had entered the COBR suite had been entirely justified. Effectively, he had blood on his hands. That, at least, was the way people would see it.

But somehow he had to keep the business of government going. Otherwise, things would be even worse. He, at least, had to give the appearance of unflappable competence. He took a deep breath. 'Thank you, Frank. That is deeply distressing. I would be grateful for a fuller and more specific report as soon as it becomes possible to provide one. In the meanwhile, I think we should hear how things stand in other respects. I'd like to start with Ofcom. Sheila: can you tell us what communication systems are now working, and what we can expect to see happening from now on?'

'Certainly, Prime Minister. The news on this front is more encouraging. You will already be aware that the mobile phone networks are now operating again in London – and indeed in most of the rest of the country – as are the fixed-fibre networks. We have full connectivity to the world wide web, and international data services have almost all been restored. So far as we have been able to ascertain, the great majority of satellites in the GNSS arrays over the UK – both GPS and Galileo – are now operating normally. And we have just heard from the broadcasters that they expect to be on air again by around noon today. National Grid tells us that domestic electricity supplies were restored in almost all parts of the country by this morning, so we are expecting that TVs (both terrestrial and satellite) will be receiving; and those using IP-based systems, whether through smart mobile technology or through PCs, should also be able to receive. So I think we can say that the country is now once again open for business both for point-to-point and for point-to-multipoint communications.'

'Thank you, Sheila. That is indeed good news. Dr Donoghue, could you give us the Bank of England's perspective on the state of the financial markets?'

Bill was ready for this – having ascertained that the Governor had been stuck in Barbados throughout the past five days, he was sure he would have to continue as the Bank's man at COBR until at least the end of the day.

'Prime Minister: you will recall that, at the start of this crisis, I predicted that there could be difficulties for global markets and global communications, owing to the overcrowding of the Internet by data packets searching fruitlessly for a way to reach London. This appears to have been exactly what did occur. I have only had brief conversations with counterparts in Singapore and Shanghai, who are of course open before our opening. My understanding from them is that they, and others who opened before our networks were largely restored this morning, closed their markets as soon as they realized that the data flow had ceased and had worked out that this was due to the black-out in London. This appears to have unclogged the Internet within a fairly short period. So the interruption of global communications was much less long-lived than I had feared. Clearly, there will be some messy transactions to try to clear up ex post, once everything has otherwise got back to normal, but at least the scale of the problems is much smaller than it would have been if this had all occurred in the midst of a normal trading period rather than over New Year. Turning to the UK domestic scene, I will be in touch with the clearing banks as soon as I return to Threadneedle Street, but I would expect them to be operating credit cards and other clearing operations as normal from this morning onwards.'

Going round the table, the picture from all departments was essentially the same. The transport system was now back to normal; the gas system was operating again. There were reports of criminal damage caused by people breaking into food shops, but these were limited, and the food supply chain would be functioning, now that purchasing was possible again.

Basically, the story was simple. The country had gone into involuntary hibernation for nearly five days in deep mid-winter. And hundreds of thousands of frail, elderly people were dead or dying as a result.

The PM knew very well what this meant. Parliament would have to be recalled for Wednesday, and he would have to announce his resignation. It was the worst civil disaster since the pandemic flu that followed the First World War – with the difference that, this time, people would want to know why there was no back-up system for communication and no pre-ordained plan for social care to reach the elderly in their homes. He couldn't explain it, except to say that the chance of this happening had been rated as low, and that the modern convergent, networked society that had let them all down so badly for five days did them all proud the rest of the time. That wasn't a message he could imagine himself giving – or at least not without falling on his sword.

As he closed the meeting and headed over to the door, he drew Bill aside: 'Dr Donoghue, I gather from my private secretary that you have lost a close relative in the midst of all this?'

'Yes, Prime Minister. My mother-in-law. Once the Governor is back this afternoon, I have to go back to Somerset and tell my wife.'

The PM nodded mutely. He knew that there are times for words and times for silence.

9

THE GLOBAL PERSPECTIVE

The parable of this book takes place in just one country – Britain. However, the issues that the parable raises are clearly global in character, because the convergent networks on which Britain's economy and society increasingly depends are replicated the world over, and many of these networks are themselves physically part of global or multinational systems. Most notably, the Internet is an intrinsically global system. Given the increasingly central role that the Internet plays in the operation of all other networks, this means that the whole world can now increasingly be regarded as depending upon an emerging, global network of networks – which gives a new meaning to the term 'globalization'.

So we should be alive to a series of questions about the international implications of network failure. Each of these questions deserves an answer, and some of them are not easy to answer.

Global differences and global similarities

The first point is that, though the issues are global, the problem is not 'the same everywhere' – because, when it comes to networks, there are lots of obvious and relevant differences between one country and another. To list just a few: different countries have different levels of Internet penetration; different levels of electrification; different degrees of centralization, regionalization or localization in particular utility networks; different transport, energy, food production, social care and healthcare systems; different arrangements for their emergency services and armed services; different banking systems with greater or smaller degrees of integration and centralization; different methods of payment for goods and services – or at least differing degrees of reliance on one payment-method or another; different dependence on global satellite networks and global telecommunications networks; and different degrees of exposure to differing climatic conditions in the event of network failures of differing kinds.

These are not just random differences. There are various (admittedly imperfect) rules of thumb about which countries are more or less likely to be exposed to catastrophic effects of system-wide network failures. Broadly, the more recently developed, the more developed, the more electronic and digital, the more centralized, and the more subject to climatic extremes a given country is, the more impact system-wide network failure is likely to have. Of course, these characteristics don't all line up in neat rows. The exposure of a given country to systemic network failures can be compared with the exposure of other countries only by constructing a sophisticated analysis that allows for all the relevant differences between countries. No doubt, if some PhD student or think-tank were painstakingly to construct such a sophisticated analysis, it would show some countries as having the lowest possible exposure, other countries as having maximal exposure, and many countries somewhere in between.

This would be an interesting study to do. But I'm not at all sure that it would be *more* than merely interesting – because, once all of the differences have been understood, the fact remains that every single country is pretty highly exposed, and every single country is likely to become more exposed over time, because of the onward march of technology.

These sound like bold assertions. Why are they plausible? In the first place, because – although there are hundreds of millions of people in various parts of the world who still don't have electricity or mains water supply or access to telecommunications – there is now no country in the world which is entirely devoid of these networks. Out of the current world population (of around 8 billion people), about 4 billion have direct access to the Internet, and about 5 billion have mobile phones. Once one allows for the fact that, in the poorest and least developed countries, there is some sharing of single items of equipment, and once one allows also for the number of very young and very old people around the world who don't have access to these services, as well as the number of people in very poor countries who live in remote rural areas, these figures mean that, even in the least developed countries, a high proportion of the working-age inhabitants of the main cities will have telecommunications and Internet access. Certainly, those who are doing the most important jobs in such countries will nowadays be relying on a range of networks, including telecommunications and the Internet (and therefore also the electricity supply networks) in their professional lives. So the functioning even of the lowest-income, least-developed countries increasingly depends upon these networks. And, of course, the march of progress ensures that electrification, telecommunications and access to the Internet are all rolling out at a high pace in many areas where they were not previously present. Accordingly, the degree of dependence upon these networks is increasing day by day throughout the world.

In short, even if some countries currently are not as network-dependent as advanced economies have become, this is all too likely to be a temporary rather than a permanent phenomenon. There is every chance that, a decade or two from now, the proliferation of converging networks will have become a universal, or very nearly universal, phenomenon. With that will come huge benefits for mankind, but also huge risks. Countries whose governments have not in the past had much reason to think about network failure will in future have as much reason to think about it as we do now. The need to develop long-term strategies for resilience and social protection in the face of network failure is becoming a global challenge.

Network failure as a cause of network failure

The next question is whether this is a global problem only in the sense of being increasingly a problem for everyone everywhere, or whether the problem is also global in the sense of being something that, like certain diseases, can spread from one country to another.

The short answer is that network failures in country A certainly can trigger network failures in country B under some circumstances.

To take a very simple case, if the energy system of country B depends upon the energy system of country A, and country A's energy networks go down, then country B's energy networks are likely to be seriously affected. If, for example, Russian gas suddenly ceases to be available to Western Europe during a cold spell because the Russian gas transmission networks fail over a sustained period for some reason, then this will have a big effect on security of electricity and gas supply in Germany and elsewhere in the European Union (EU), since the EU imports just under 40% of its gas from Russia. But these sorts of effect are limited – because Germany, which would be worst hit, has already constructed gas reserves capable of keeping the German gas network fully supplied for more than two months, during which time more liquid natural gas could be imported from other parts of the world.

Similarly, as the fabric of electricity interconnection within Europe and between different 'pools' or states and provinces in the USA and Canada increases (with massive economic advantages, and also with advantages for security of supply under all normal circumstances), the exposure of one European country, American state or Canadian province to serious interruptions of electricity supply in another country, state or province increases. But here, too, the individual entities have typically built their electricity supply networks in ways that will ensure they can 'get by' even under such circumstances, because they maintain sufficient 'capacity margins' of spare generating plant to make up for the electricity which they couldn't, under these circumstances, import.

The situation is much more worrying when we turn to telecommunications and the Internet, and to the multitude of activities (such as banking) that fundamentally depend upon these global networks.

In all sorts of ways, the Internet (and the telecoms

networks built upon its protocols) are global systems. The packets of data that traverse the Internet follow kaleidoscopic pathways, as they seek out the destinations at which they can be reunited with their original comrades to re-form intelligible messages, traversing diverse geographies determined by the dynamics of the net. If there are blockages along one route, the packages are diverted to other routes, sometimes boomeranging from continent to continent. (Indeed, it is this boomerang effect that can cause massive traffic-jams if enough parts of the net become unavailable at any one time.)

Some of these effects can be constrained if there is a problem in a particular part of the global network of networks. For example, if a server in another continent or country becomes inaccessible because the pathways to it are blocked by network failure, the result may simply be that I am unable to access a piece of information that it would be useful for me to have – an inconvenience, but hardly a disaster.

However, the fact that businesses of all sorts all around the world now depend on being able to download data and apps from the Internet means that failure to access a server in a distant land may increasingly become a major problem for the provision of a particular service in my own country. The analogy, here, is with the physical just-in-time supply chains for industries like motor manufacturing, which hugely increases their financial efficiency in normal times, but exposes them to larger risks in the event of quite small supply interruptions.

But the significance of electronic network failure goes way beyond the problems generated by interruptions of physical supply chains. The most extreme example of this phenomenon is in the global financial markets. The events in our parable helpfully occur at a time of year when the whole world's markets are shut. But if the same things were to happen at a time when the markets were functioning, then a welter of global transactions would fail – leaving a huge trail of imponderable consequences for transactions across the world. It could take months or even years to sort out the mess.

For all of these reasons, we should regard the global communications system as a highly integrated whole. Attacks on its integrity at any location constitute potential attacks on its integrity at all locations. In this sense, at least, the world is truly becoming an electronic village.

Common and divergent interests

This leads us on to another, even more important, question: whether all countries share a common interest in the stability of the emerging global network of networks, or whether there are asymmetries that create differing interests for different countries.

The issues here are very difficult and very profound.

They reach to the core of the international rules-based system, which has been gradually established since the time of the First World War, was essentially given its current shape after the Second World War, and is now under severe strain as a result of the rise of an alternative international system centred on China, India and Russia.

We can see this most clearly if we turn our attention away from networks for a moment, and look instead at the rules and institutions developed to tame armed conflicts after the massacres of 1914–18 and 1939–45. The architecture of these international rules and institutions has a dual aspect. Its outer walls are designed to protect the common interests of all nations; but the rooms within are designed to accommodate the diverging interests of differing nations and regimes. The various elements of the rules-based order – the United Nations Convention on the Law of the Sea, International Humanitarian Law and the Geneva Convention, the Vienna Convention, the International Criminal Court, the International Court at The Hague, the 1951 Refugee Convention, and so forth – aim to regulate the actions of governments in a way that minimizes the damage to individual countries and to humanity arising from global conflict, while at the same time recognizing that under certain circumstances there will be such conflict.

These international conventions and multi-lateral bodies do not prevent war, or inter-state espionage, or efforts by one state to interfere in the affairs of another; but they do set ground-rules which, if observed, reduce the horror of war and limit the extent and nature of the espionage and interference. By allowing in this way for the possibility of conflict-under-rules, the conventions establish a bulwark against the ghastly prospect of total war. They also create a reasonably stable system of co-operation in peacetime against common enemies such as disease, natural disaster and terrorism. And they provide mechanisms for states to resolve disputes (wherever possible) in an orderly and peaceable manner without resort to warfare.

What holds true for the traditional international relationships of the past and present will basically hold true also for the network relationships of the present and future. Just as in the realm of physical conflict and physical interference involving troops on the ground, so in the realm of global networks there are both common interests and conflicting interests. Nations, collectively, have an interest in protecting their networks against natural disaster, international criminal activity, terrorism and the like. But, alongside these common interests in stability, individual nations may think that they can make gains for their own citizens and their own regimes by attempting to use global networks against other states. Some of the examples of cyber-attack to which I have referred in a previous chapter very clearly come into this latter category;

and there is almost certainly also a large amount of global cyber-espionage that has the same character.

So the real issue is which of these two contrary trends comes to dominate the thinking of individual governments and of the international community as a whole at any given moment. To the extent that individual governments hope to be able to exercise power over other nations through the scope for attack on their networks, they will tend to resist any international moves towards a proliferation of analogue fallback options that would increase resilience to such attack. But, to the extent that each government is thinking about their own (and the common) interest in maintaining stability in the face of technical failure, natural disaster, crime or terrorism, they will tend to favour international efforts to make analogue fallback options universal.

This is a much more vexed issue than, for example, climate change – where, despite all the complexities of negotiating an international framework for emissions control, there is at least a common acceptance that climate change is a problem for all nations, and there is no suggestion that any one nation can use it directly as a means of establishing or increasing power over another nation. In dealing with the protection of populations against the effects of prolonged network failure, the position is much more equivocal because of the temptation for certain states to welcome the possibility of such network failure in certain other states as a means of establishing global competitive advantage or even hegemony. But somehow, we surely need – for the sake of humanity as a whole – to find a means of focusing the minds of governments around the world on the common interest that we all have in ensuring that we are not all adversely affected by network failure of a kind that none of us wants and that none of us has intentionally caused. And this level of global protection against the worst effects of prolonged, systemic network failure can be achieved only if we join together to ensure that each country on Earth has basic analogue fallback options. Only in this way, can we each prevent crises from turning into cataclysms in our own countries, and prevent crises in one country from creating cataclysms in another country.

Constructing global solutions

But can we turn the minds of all governments in this direction, so that they focus on common interests and universal fallback protections, instead of participating in a deadly game of beggar-my-neighbour? There is no point in being naïve about this. It is not going to be easy – because the politics aren't easy. But there are ways of playing judo with this problem: in other words, ways of using the weight of the problem to bring about the solution.

Even though the eventual goal is cooperation and the

protection of common interests, we need to start with competition and self-interest. Without so much as mentioning the rest of the world, we can seek to persuade government in our own country to take all the steps necessary to establish and maintain in good working order all of the analogue fallback options that are needed to give us some protection against the effects of network failure in a digital age. This, from the point of view of the first government that does it (quite possibly the British government), is an act of pure national self-interest. It also creates a clear competitive advantage vis-à-vis other countries. The country that first has adequate fallback arrangements in place is the country that is least exposed to being subdued or blackmailed by network attack, whether from terrorists or criminals or other states; and it is also the country best protected against the network-induced effects of natural disaster. But, paradoxically, this first mover is taking a morally benign step – because it is creating a competitive incentive for other governments to follow suit, to the advantage of their own populations. And, as the number of countries that join the fallback-option club grows, so does the incentive for yet others to join the club too, in order to avoid being more vulnerable than their friends and enemies.

We can in this way hope, by slow degrees, to tip the world as a whole into something near to universal adoption of fallback options.

Constructing global mechanisms

Once the competitive dynamics of enlightened self-interest have begun to produce this benign result, it will no longer be naïve to hope that something more durable and predictable can be built – in the form of a new extension to the architecture of international rules and institutions.

The starting point will be a new convention on global network protection to parallel the United Nations Convention on the Law of the Sea or the Geneva conventions on international humanitarian law. What this new convention needs to set out is at least:

— the right of all states to defend their networks against attack from all-comers, whether other states, non-state actors or nature itself;

— the obligation of all states to protect their citizens by constructing fallback options that will permit ordinary life to continue under circumstances in which networks have failed for whatever reasons;

— the obligation of rich states to assist poor states through overseas development assistance both to enhance the defences of their networks and to develop fallback options as a protection against the effects of network failure; and

— the applicability of existing international law

obligations not to make unprovoked attack
against networks, in order to put beyond doubt
that such an attack is a form of warfare which is
governed by the rules of warfare.

As with the other major international conventions,
we will need also a new institution through which the
international community as a whole can monitor compliance with the new convention and, to the extent possible,
enforce the rules contained within the convention. The
natural location for such an institution is within the
United Nations family. And the shape of the institution
should probably be modelled more on the International
Atomic Energy Agency than on the International Criminal Court, since the aim here is not so much to convict
and punish the aggressors but rather to foster international cooperation through a formal mechanism for
agreeing rules and monitoring compliance.

The forums in which it would be natural to promote
and debate the establishment of this new international
architecture are the United Nations General Assembly,
the United Nations Security Council and the G20 group
of leading world economies. In all of these, Britain has not
only a place but also a leading (some might argue, an overweight) role. So it would be natural for Britain, as an early
mover in both network defence and in the construction of
network fallback options, to take the initiative (as it has

done, to huge effect, in moving the world to tackle both the scourge of anti-microbial resistance and the dangers of climate change).

The right time to begin this global work is now – because these things take a long time to accomplish, and time is short.

The risk of complacency

But can we actually make this all happen soon? Or will every effort to forge a new international consensus fail until we experience a real network disaster somewhere in the world?

The evidence from the historical record is mixed. In cases like anti-microbial resistance and climate change, it has proved possible to mobilize intensive international concern *before* any disaster occurs. But in other cases such as the financial crash of 2008 (and indeed the Great Depression of 1929 before that), there was no serious international effort to reduce the huge risks caused by excessive debt and inflated asset prices until they crystallized into huge disasters, even though these risks were staring everybody in the face for years before the disasters occurred; indeed, some commentators argue that debt levels remain at dangerously high levels even now.

What process should we follow to maximize the chance of the world's governments sitting up and taking notice before they are forced to do so by a crisis of the sort we are trying to avert?

Part of the answer to this question lies in recognizing that the process of strategic diplomacy is incremental: it consists of rolling the stone along, and along and along, until it eventually gathers enough moss to become an irresistibly large object of international attention. The long history of global progress on climate change and greenhouse gas emissions is instructive here. When the issue was first placed on the agenda at relevant international gatherings, it was regarded as somewhat eccentric and of dubious scientific validity – a case of scaremongering by an eccentric fringe. Gradually, however, as the Intergovernmental Panel on Climate Change was established to validate the science, and as the United Nations Framework Convention on Climate Change was used as the engine to organize regular, formal Conferences of the Parties (twenty-two of them so far, and with more to come), the whole process acquired a very considerable momentum of its own. As it did so, the question subtly and gradually transmuted from 'whether there are serious risks caused by anthropogenic climate change' to 'whether to do something about the risks of climate change', and then into the question 'what to do to reduce the risks of climate change' before finally becoming 'how much to do to reduce the risks of climate change'.

In a similar way, global leaders will now need to begin by placing on the agenda the question whether there are serious risks arising for humanity from network failure – a question that this book seeks to answer, but which many other books, articles, papers and studies will need to address before it is taken sufficiently seriously. Then there will need to be discussion of an institutional structure for considering the issues – very possibly a United Nations Framework Convention on Network Failure. This will, in turn, need to be followed by the establishment of some analogue to the Conferences of the Parties and to the Intergovernmental Panel that have, in relation to climate change, so successfully provided both a forum for discussion of practical measures and a structure for achieving consensus on the science. These institutions will gradually enable the governments of the world to develop a menu of options for the protection of networks and for reversion to analogue fallback provision in the event of network failure. The existence of such a global framework will also promote increasing understanding of (and hence permit the gradual forging of a global consensus on) the risks that are likely to arise as the various network technologies develop and converge.

What we are talking about, here, is not a moment or a flash of inspiration but the grindingly slow, incremental, progressive implementation of a long-term strategy.

But if efforts are made through global cooperation of the enlightened to set this strategy in place – and if, crucially, there are simultaneously some countries that are demonstrably gaining a competitive advantage by leading the way towards the construction of effective network defences and effective fallback options for themselves – then it is possible that frameworks can be set in place before we prove the need for them through encountering a real-life form of our parable.

There is one further significant geopolitical point that needs to be made here. We are probably on the eve of a new global politics in which China and India will regain something like the 50% share of global GDP that they had for millennia before the Industrial Revolution dramatically changed Western productivity and hence Western levels of income and power. And we can already see very clearly the leading role that China and India are playing in the high-tech industries that will be at the core of future networks. No company in the world is more important than China's Huawei to the development of communications networks, nor is any company in the world more important than India's Tata Communications to the development of the software on which network capabilities rest. Nowhere in the world is the use of the Internet more fully evolved than in China and India. Never before in the history of the world have new networks of every kind been built as in China over the last three decades;

and the Indians are now gearing up to do something very similar. All in all, the age of China and India that is now approaching will be not only a network-centric age, but also one in which China and India themselves (as well as gaining increasing geopolitical dominance) become physically and virtually central to the global network of networks.

The need for a long-term strategy leading to the establishment of a new international framework for global network protection presents not only a major challenge but also a major opportunity. This can become one element of the international rules-based order which (unlike the rest of the international treaties, conventions and institutions) is fashioned at least partly, and maybe even mainly, by the Easterners. By this means, meeting the challenge of global network failure can become an opportunity to bind the two emerging super-powers of the East into the concept and practice of an evolving international order, to the considerable advantage of the whole of mankind.

We must surely seize that opportunity. The message of this book is that we cannot afford, either within our own national boundaries or across the world, to place our faith solely in the capacity of technology itself to prevent the unexpected from occurring. As we stand on the threshold of what are probably the most fundamental and product-ive technological transformations in human history, the only way to ensure the continued acceptance of those transformations is for us to work together to develop new forms of resilience that rely on the establishment of simple, 'analogue' fallback options. The human cost of not doing so could be very high indeed.

INDEX

INDEX